Praise

'If you're going to succeed in the Entrepreneur Revolution, you're going to need technology that delivers results. This book is a treasure trove of insights for modern entrepreneurs. It offers a clear path to leveraging technology for business success. It's a must-have for anyone serious about scaling their business in today's fast-paced environment.'
— **Daniel Priestley**, CEO, Dent Global, and author of *Entrepreneur Revolution*

'Paul McGillivray has crafted a brilliant guide with *Scope to Scale*. This book empowers business leaders to reclaim their time and focus on what truly matters. It's an engaging and practical read for anyone who wants to get out of the weeds – which is all of us!'
— **Sháá Wasmund MBE**, businesswoman, author, educator and one of the *Sunday Times* Top 20 Most Influential Entrepreneurs in the UK

'Paul McGillivray's *Scope to Scale* is a game-changer for anyone committed to operational excellence. This book is well written and easy to read, and the straightforward, actionable SCOPE framework makes the complex task of business systemisation both achievable and painless. As a champion of consistent operational excellence, I can vouch for this book as an essential resource for anyone who is serious about scaling their business effectively.'

— **Marianne Page**, operational excellence and peak performance specialist, and bestselling author of *Simple, Logical, Repeatable*

'In *Scope to Scale*, Paul McGillivray provides a clear and practical roadmap for business leaders. His insights into automation and systemisation are both innovative and highly effective. This book is a must-read for anyone serious about driving operational excellence and long-term growth.'

— **Paul Avins**, host of the *ScaleUp* podcast and author of *Secrets of the Business Wealth Accelerators*

'As a startup founder, I can say that *Scope to Scale* is the bomb. It's a total game-changer for anyone looking to harness the power of technology to drive income and innovation or enhance social impact. Paul has this incredible ability to take the complex world of tech scalability and make it not just understandable but exciting. It's like having a brilliant CTO in your pocket, guiding you through the digital landscape with clarity and vision.'

— **Natalie Jameson**, Senior Vice President, Bank of New York; Founder, Heroworx; and inventor of YZen.AI

SCOPE TO SCALE

Drive your business success
through the power of
supportive software systems

PAUL MCGILLIVRAY

R^ethink

First published in Great Britain in 2024
by Rethink Press (www.rethinkpress.com)

© Copyright Paul McGillivray

To Jeannie. My heart, my soul, my partner in all things.

To Ella. Your kind heart, and creative spirit inspire me every day. The incredible person you are fills me with pride and gratitude.

Contents

Foreword

There's a moment when every business leader stands at the edge of the known, poised between the comfort of what is familiar and the potential of what could be. For leaders who understand the value of software systems to support them as they step into the unknown territory of their next chapter, *Scope to Scale* by Paul McGillivray provides reassuring guidance and a companion with which to navigate the journey ahead. It is both practical and visionary – a work that perfectly mirrors the character of its author.

I have had the privilege of knowing Paul for over thirty years. Our journey together, both in life and in business, has been marked by challenges and moments of profound growth and discovery that have shaped who we are today. We created Remote, our award-winning software development studio, and have led it side-by-side for almost as long as we have known one another. During that time, I've seen first-hand Paul's extraordinary gift for turning complex digital challenges into clearly articulated opportunities for transformation time and again. What sets Paul apart – and what makes this book so valuable – is his ability to see how technology can be harnessed to serve humanity and craft solutions that work for people in meaningful ways.

Paul's approach has always been about more than just creating systems or implementing software. From the beginning, he has understood that technology must serve a greater purpose. It should empower people, amplify their potential and drive positive impact across entire organisations. He has kept pace with the technological shifts that have shaped our world and actively cultivated practical ways that businesses can harness those advances to create a culture of innovation and growth. It's a passion that has lasted the test of time. His vision for Remote and the businesses we've worked with has always been rooted in the idea that technology should be a force for good, for sustainable, purposeful evolution.

Running a business like Remote has allowed us to work with some of the world's most recognised brands – Sony, Volvo and VW, to name a few. In each project Paul has led, he has demonstrated his rare talent for understanding the intricate mechanics of business systems and the broader vision of what those systems can achieve. His real genius, though, lies in his ability to communicate these ideas in ways anyone can grasp. I've often marvelled at how Paul can take concepts as complex as AI, Agile methodology or business automation and make them accessible, even inspiring, for a diverse audience of business leaders, teams and clients.

In *Scope to Scale*, Paul shares the essence of what makes him such an effective leader and visionary. The SCOPE framework he introduces is more than a technical roadmap – it reflects his core belief that businesses can and should grow with purpose. This framework highlights opportunities for efficiencies and potential for automation which create systems that allow leaders to navigate the digital age and stay true to their values. It's about building a foundation for scalable, sustainable growth that honours both the organisation and the people within it.

As Paul discusses in this book, automation is often seen as a way to free up time and resources or to make businesses more profitable, and while that's true, the deeper power of automation is that it unlocks human potential. By automating the mundane, companies can allow their teams to focus on innovation, creativity and other high-value activities that drive real progress. The case studies included in this book show the real-world impact of Paul's work, from revolutionising stock management to transforming operational efficiency in industries as diverse as manufacturing, finance and health. But beyond the numbers and outcomes, these stories illustrate how technology, when implemented with purpose, changes the very culture of an organisation, empowering people to thrive.

Paul can see beyond a project's immediate needs and anticipate the future. He solves the immediate problems while building systems that continue delivering value for years. His work is always forward-thinking and grounded in the belief that the true measure of success lies in both the immediate gains and long-term, sustainable growth that benefits everyone involved.

For any values-led business leader looking to scale their business in a way that honours both their purpose and their people, *Scope to Scale* is an invaluable resource. It provides the tools and strategies for navigating the complexities of digital transformation and the clarity and confidence needed to do so with integrity. Paul's vision is both ambitious and achievable, and this book is a testament to his ability to inspire others to embrace that vision for themselves.

As Paul's partner in life and business, I am deeply honoured to write the foreword for this remarkable work. *Scope to Scale* will undoubtedly become a cornerstone for leaders who understand that growth is not just about scaling their business but also their impact in the world.

Jeannie McGillivray
CEO and Co-founder, Remote

Introduction

I t's clear to everyone that the new wave of technology-driven business is well and truly here. The future of work is now, and as a smart, aware business leader, you need to embrace this revolution before it leaves you and your company behind.

The tech unicorns like Google, Facebook and Amazon hit our headlines on a regular basis, because of their ethics and abuse of their technology nearly as much as the huge amounts of money and power that technology is helping them to generate. There's another revolution going on in businesses around the world, though; a smaller, quieter, less well-known or glamorous one, but it's possibly more impactful and world-changing than the magical feats performed by the Gods of Silicon Valley.

As cloud computing, artificial intelligence (AI), powerful code frameworks and community-led learning become more and more pervasive and accessible, organisations all over the world are harnessing software automation to get their time back, to reduce the repetitive admin work that consumes most businesses and to get much more done. They delight many more customers, consistently and reliably, and make far greater profits while doing so, without needing to hire more staff.

Those same businesses are then finding that they have the headspace to innovate ideas for products and services that they can scale to bring in regular revenue streams from excited and enthusiastic new customers. As a result, something remarkable is happening. In offices all over the world, business leaders are beginning to look inwards and examine *why* they do what they do, rediscovering their values, bringing meaning to their lives and those of their employees, and asking themselves afresh how they can thrive in this rapidly changing new environment.

This is a book about building software, but it's not about coding. Most business owners are experts in their own industry, but not in technology. Whether it's providing a new or existing service online or a business workflow system that will streamline their operations, they usually know what they need and have a good sense that technology can meet that need, but they don't know how to go about driving the process to get it built.

That's where I come in with my software development studio, Remote. I founded the studio with my wife and partner in all things, Jeannie, back in 1999. We lead a team of expert strategists mapping out the grand plan, designers weaving creativity, developers breathing life into ideas and product specialists finetuning for ultimate user satisfaction. For us, it's not just about writing code – it's about chasing excellence, about getting better every single day, about building software that makes a measurable impact on the people who use it. We collaborate closely with our clients on our projects; we study each business inside out, audit its processes, identify the opportunities for software to elevate it, and then we design and build that software.

As cofounder and chief technology officer (CTO) of Remote, I've spent the last twenty-five years working with over 200 clients, each with their own ambitions and challenges. Together, we've increased their profits and freed up their time and resources through the magic of software, often reimagining their business by innovating brand-new digital products and services.

Through years of iteration and innovation, my team and I have developed a tried-and-tested approach to ensure the success and empowerment of every software project we undertake, delivering a significant return on investment (ROI) for our clients. The result, the SCOPE framework, is the centrepiece of this book, offering you an opportunity to join the automation revolution with confidence.

This book serves as a roadmap as you reassess your business, strategise your next steps and embark on a new journey towards success, freedom and financial health. Its focus is on using custom software to optimise business operations.

A smooth and efficient business operation is crucial before you branch out to new services or expand your team to create even more impact. Optimised, effective operations provide the foundations for all business growth, creating a stable framework within which to scale while supporting every team member in their role so that they can focus on the work they're great at rather than the necessary administration that often surrounds that work. This book will walk you through the process, so that when you build software systems in your own business, you'll be empowered as you'll understand what happens, when it happens and why.

Here's how we'll do it. In Part One, I'll introduce you to the ways that software can automate your business processes and workflow. We'll talk about the true meaning of disruption in the business technology sense and how the various methods I'm going to show you can turn you into an innovation machine, inventing new ways to reach and delight your customers, and making your income more stable and reliable than ever before. Part One lays out the foundations for a new way of working, so you'll finish it with a good understanding of the importance and urgency of embracing the revolution, and be ready to get started.

Part Two is where we get stuck in. I'll walk you through the SCOPE framework, which will be your map to this new territory.

The SCOPE framework consists of five sections:

1. **Strategise.** It all starts with digital strategy. We deep dive into systems thinking and the theory of constraints. By the end of 'Strategise', you'll understand what needs to change and have a view of the big picture when it comes to your business.

2. **Clarify.** This stage is about calculating the way forward, getting a clear view of where you're at. You'll map out your business workflows to understand them from a different level. I'll share with you a suite of tools you can use to identify bottlenecks in your business and opportunities to automate, while aligning with your larger goals.

3. **Optimise.** Here, you'll refine your workflows. You'll map out your ideal customer and team journeys, and build the path to a brighter and more impactful future for your organisation. We'll also talk about an essential concept of successful software development: the minimum viable product (MVP). You'll learn how to keep your project lean and focused on the most important outcomes.

4. **Prototype.** With the key concepts in place, you'll work on the visual side of things, learning how a clickable prototype can let you test and adjust

your assumptions before anyone's written a line of code. You'll explore different types of prototypes and the importance of user testing throughout the development process.

5. **Execute.** Now things get real; the execution of a successful software delivery is hard, but there's a tried-and-trusted way to ensure that this most essential part of your journey falls into what we at Remote term 'low risk, high adventure'. For many people who do it the wrong way, this stage can be a nightmare. You'll learn how to ensure that it's smooth, pain-free, effective and perhaps even fun. You'll discover ways to calculate your ROI before you get started, so that you can progress with confidence. You'll also dive into the principles of Agile development and why it's crucial for modern software projects.

When people think of automation and software performing the jobs that so many do manually right now, they often imagine a soulless enterprise laying off employees and filling empty offices with the sound of computers taking over our lives. In my experience, the contrary is true. Used correctly, software empowers the people who drive it; it enables them to find meaning in their work and spend time doing tasks they enjoy and are good at; it builds momentum, increases reach and creates an energy in an organisation that is both exciting and uplifting.

It's not about doing the same amount of work with half of the workforce. It's about the same workforce getting twice as much done with less effort, leading to happier team members and customers who sing your praises from the rooftops.

The software revolution

Embracing new technologies can drive innovation and ensure sustained business growth. Failing to adapt to those new technologies can quickly lead to obsolescence. The business landscape is filled with recent examples of companies that have either risen to prominence or fallen into obscurity as a result of their ability or failure to embrace technological change. These contemporary stories serve as powerful lessons for today's business leaders.

In the logistics sector, DHL has successfully embraced digital transformation by implementing AI and smart glasses technology to optimise warehouse operations. It has also introduced solutions to streamline vital processes, automate repetitive tasks and help its teams become more productive. These solutions include autonomous guided vehicles to enhance operations, chatbots to complement customer service operations and shipment sensors with track-and-trace capabilities (DHL, 2019, 2021).

The financial services sector has also seen dramatic shifts. Traditional banks, burdened by legacy systems and bureaucratic inertia, have struggled to compete with fintech startups like Revolut and Robinhood. These agile companies leverage AI, blockchain and other cutting-edge technologies to offer seamless, user-friendly financial services. The rapid adoption of digital wallets and cryptocurrencies has further challenged established financial institutions to innovate or risk becoming irrelevant.

The healthcare industry, too, is experiencing a technological revolution, thanks to companies like Teladoc. While traditional healthcare providers have been hesitant to fully embrace telemedicine, Teladoc has utilised AI-driven diagnostics and virtual consultations to meet the growing demand for remote healthcare services, particularly during the pandemic. This shift has redefined patient care and set new benchmarks for the industry.

In the legal sector, Lawtech UK is driving significant change. This initiative, backed by the Ministry of Justice, aims to innovate legal services delivery through the adoption of AI and custom software solutions. By implementing these technologies, law firms have improved client service, increased operational efficiency and enhanced data security, positioning the UK as a leader in legal tech innovation.

The message is clear: the ability to swiftly adapt to technological advancements is vital. Companies that embrace these changes can revolutionise their operations and enhance customer experiences. Those who hesitate risk becoming the next cautionary tale.

We must be ready to let go of outdated practices and embrace innovation. By doing so, we can thrive in our industry, staying ahead of the competition and continuously evolving. We must do this increasingly often as technology's progress rapidly accelerates. Recognising and *becoming* the disruption – learning to disrupt ourselves as our method of business – needs to be our new modus operandi, or we will join the disrupted and the broken, the Kodaks and the Blockbusters. Software projects can be challenging, expensive and sometimes a massive money pit, but done correctly, they can provide a huge ROI and transform an organisation. Software allows us to dream big, step into those dreams and bring them to life. Join me as I show you how to make that happen successfully.

I've written this book to help you ensure your business leverages the latest technological advancements, so that you become a leader in your field. By embracing innovation and staying ahead of the curve, you'll set the standards for success in your industry and create an environment in which others follow your lead. In the following pages, I'll walk you through the processes I've developed over more than twenty-five years of working with clients of all sizes, from tech startups all the way through to corporate giants.

Clients of Remote have embraced the transformative power of software. They're automating processes, creating streamlined workflows, reducing delivery times, generating insightful reports and crafting interactive portals for customers and teams. They're revolutionising product use, learning and buying experiences, and continually reshaping their businesses for the digital age.

In doing so, they've saved themselves time and money, and stayed ahead of their competition.

They've made more sales, acquired new customers and increased their capacity to serve and delight the ones they already had. Collectively, they've saved and made (conservatively) tens of millions of pounds in doing so.

Doing this requires a new way of thinking about the problems the world of business is facing. You don't need to run a giant corporation investing millions into the latest idea to stand a chance at becoming a world leader in your industry. Repeatedly, the Remote team has seen startups and spinoffs redefine 'normal' in an industry. It happens so subtly and stealthily that to a casual observer, these disruptions can look like simple and obvious evolutions.

They're not. They're the result of strong and capable strategy, of specific methods being applied at the right time, of business leaders having the courage to step up, to take a chance and to invest in doing something differently.

Now it's your time to join those leaders. Let's get started...

PART ONE
THE ROBOTS ARE COMING

1
The Origin Of The Robot

On 25 January 1921, Czech playwright and journalist Karel Čapek premiered his latest play to the world. Set in the year 2000, *Rossumovi Univerzální Roboti* (or *Rossum's Universal Robots*) was the story of a company that created artificial biological organisms that looked like humans, could think for themselves and could carry out chores that humans didn't want to do. They could do everything that humans could... except love (Čapek, 1923).

Rossum's universal robots had no soul. They were the unfeeling workforce that existed to serve the humans, and as you can imagine, they were incredibly popular, becoming the core of the army and manual labour. They quickly became a necessity worldwide, working for free and manufacturing products at a fifth of the cost of human labourers. The economy became robot-based and the robots could all communicate with each other, regardless of nationality or language. In choosing the word 'robot', based on the Old Church Slavonic *robota*, meaning 'servitude', 'forced labour' or 'drudgery', Čapek created the idea of a legion of synthetic workers at the command of humanity. In the play, amidst calls for robot rights and pay, the artificial serfs revolt and all but wipe out the human race. The same play that birthed and named the idea of a robot workforce simultaneously instilled in us the fear of a robot revolution – our uneasy relationship with automation was born (Jordan, 2019).

Software exists to make our lives easier and to do the mundane tasks for us so that we don't have to. The promise of automation is more free time; revenue while we sleep; less stress; more productivity. The reality of this promise is one of work becoming increasingly demanding; the tech giants becoming more powerful while smaller businesses are pushed out; demands from clients getting greater as expectations are raised by high-performing success stories; and the risk of disruption to our own companies. At the same time, we feel that our jobs are at risk, and new advancements in technology are greeted with an equal measure of wonder and suspicion.

There are some cold hard facts that we need to face head-on here. Yes, the robots are coming. The tech giants will most likely continue to become more powerful, and software and robotics will increase their abilities to perform the tasks that we have to do on a daily basis. Software can already answer our emails, adjust our calendars to make our days more productive, write essays and reports, create spreadsheets and presentations from those reports, find and reserve spots for us in our favourite restaurants, research topics, converse with us on behalf of academic bodies of work, discover and utilise trends in data that we can't spot, create and edit photos and videos from simple text prompts, and carry out online tasks faster and more accurately than 100 humans could do manually.

It's frightening when I put it like that, but it's what's happening. The only way we can truly thrive in this new world is by looking deeply into the phenomenon and understanding the dangers and – excitingly – the opportunities. When we know the realities of both, we can avoid the former and ride the latter.

Yes, industries will continue to be disrupted, and your industry is not immune to that disruption. On the contrary – every industry is in a period of massive disruption thanks to software. Knowing this, you can stay ahead of the curve and become the disruptive influence that you may otherwise fear.

In American TV network Home Box Office's series *Breaking Bad*, character Walter White's wife confronts him after hearing of a local crime – a neighbour has been shot dead by a gunman who knocked on his door. Suspecting that Walter is up to no good, she begs him to stop whatever it is he's doing, because who knows whether someone might come knocking for him next.

Walter simply replies, 'I am the one who knocks.'

I write this with a glint in my eye and my tongue in my cheek, but I think you get the message...

Using Moore's law

If we're to harness the power available to us in the form of technology, it's important we understand the nature of that power and where it's taking us. What is the future of tech? To do that, we need to look to the past.

In 1965, Intel co-founder Gordon Moore noticed that the number of transistors per square inch on a chip doubled every year, while the cost of making the chip halved. He predicted that this trend could continue for ten years or so. It actually continued until around 2016, when the doubling of power and halving of costs slowed to the current trend of every eighteen months (Computer History Museum, no date).

The consequences of this law have been astonishing. When Apollo 11 landed on the moon in 1969, it was powered by the Apollo Guidance Computer (AGC), which had 4K of RAM and a single-core processor running at an effective instruction rate of 1.024MHz, made up of approximately 17,000 transistors. The AGC was developed at Massachusetts Institute of Technology and was ten years ahead of its time; its advanced technology was pioneering during its era (Shirriff, 2019).

Fast-forward to 2018, and the iPhone X had an A11 chip with six cores, two of them running at 2.39GHz and four of them running at 1.42GHz. All six cores could run at the same time, and the A11 chip contained 4.3 billion transistors. The iPhone X had 3GB of random-access memory (RAM) (Apple, 2017).

Just five years later, the iPhone 14 Pro had 6GB of RAM, an A16 chip with two performance cores running at 3.46GHz, four efficiency cores running at 2.02GHz, five GPU cores and a sixteen-core neural engine for AI. The A16 chip features 16 billion transistors and the neural engine is capable of nearly 17 trillion operations per second (Apple, 2022).

That last element is a critical differentiator. We're looking at a significant increase in power in just the last five years. By my (well, my AI assistant's) maths, that means the iPhone 14 Pro's 6GB was 1,573,741 times more RAM than the AGC's 4KB. The AGC cost $150,000 to build in 1966 ($1,404,659 in today's money) (Hanlon, 2017), whereas the iPhone 14's launch price was $799 for the 128GB model (Faulkner, 2022).

Even the mammoth IBM System/360 Model 75s supercomputer that controlled the landing from the Goddard Space Flight Center, which cost $3.5 million to buy ($29 million in today's money), didn't even come close to the processing power of our current smartphones (Apollo11Space, no date; Mori, 2019; IBM, no date). With the iPhone 14, not only did the addition of the neural engine add more operations per second, but it's what it *does* with those operations that is the biggest game changer to business since the advent of the PC. What AI can achieve with those 17 trillion operations per second gives us exponentially more possibilities than simply being able to do more in less time with something that fits in our pocket. More on that later.

The march of technology has been incredibly impressive, but what does that mean to us in real life, today? When we take a process that we perform manually and find a way to automate it using technology, the speed of today's computers means that the reduction in the time and cost to perform that process is huge. Thanks to Moore's law, that speed will be doubled every eighteen months, so if we have a delivery method that's digitised and automated with computer power, we'll be able to double our output, or double the number of people we can service, every eighteen months. Every product that jumps on to technology as its platform gets the ongoing boost from Moore's law, disrupts its industry and annihilates its competitors.

The digital camera destroyed the film camera industry, putting Kodak, the industry leader, out of business twenty-five years after it was developed. The technologies that are coming of age now – AI; cloud computing; natural voice recognition; text, image and video generation; 3D printing; virtual and augmented reality – are all either beginning to disrupt or already disrupting multiple industries.

Our choice is either to try to compete with those who are utilising these technologies, or to use them ourselves to gain a huge advantage. The beauty of systemising our processes is that once we've done so, we're free from having to perform those tasks ourselves, so we can work on that which aligns with our highest values – the work we love to do. What we're also doing is leveraging Moore's law to ensure that those tasks are done more quickly than we could do them manually, and increasingly so as time goes by. Our systems start off working quickly, but we then witness the exponential growth, capability and complexity of those systems, so that they perform way beyond what we could achieve on our own.

It makes sense, then, to systemise as much as possible. It'll mean we need to employ fewer staff to achieve astonishing results, and we can scale our businesses and work hugely without needing to grow into corporate behemoths with tens of thousands of employees. Importantly, the team members we do have will be freed up to work to their strongest abilities – their superpowers – so that whatever they're working on, they're bringing their best to the job, finding it fulfilling and providing real value to our organisations and customers. When team members find their work meaningful and satisfying, they tend to stay longer with an organisation, reducing expensive staff turnover.

Systems play a crucial role here, too – without them, departing employees take their knowledge with them. However, with well-implemented systems, your business's intellectual property (IP) is documented, making onboarding more affordable. More importantly, if you decide to sell your business, this codified IP significantly increases its value, acting as a powerful asset.

The singularity

AI is increasingly outperforming humans in areas such as finance, law, surgery and even the arts. Innovations like 3D printing, cloud computing, software as a service (SaaS), mobile apps and workflow automation are revolutionising business. These tools are now affordable and accessible to everyone, not just big corporations.

We can talk to our phones and they can understand us and respond. We can perform comprehensive analysis of unimaginable amounts of data, and use that analysis to predict and report, forming correlations that the human brain cannot comprehend.

Futurist Ray Kurzweil now predicts that by 2029, AI will achieve human-level intelligence, a milestone previously forecasted for 2045 (Kurzweil, 2006; SXSW, 2024). This will mark the onset of the 'singularity', an era when AI and humans merge, expanding our cognitive abilities and potentially achieving radical life extension.

In this era, technological advancements will scale beyond our imagination and grow at a pace so fast and vast, predicting the future will be like conjuring magic. We can't fully envision how our businesses will transform, but history suggests that to thrive, we must ride this growth wave instead of resisting or evading it. Adopting software systems turbocharges our business growth. As computer processing power surges, so does our capacity to magnify impact. With a burgeoning audience and constant high-quality service, we see expanding profit margins, static costs and increased leisure time. This new paradigm replaces the old way of boosting revenue by expanding our workforce, which escalated costs, diminished profit margins and complicated internal communication to the point where team members were strangers.

Embracing automation offers all the benefits outlined in this chapter, but it also calls for a change in our attitude and the way we think. The first step is really understanding the profound significance of this change and recognising the inevitable repercussions if we don't adjust.

2
Why Should
We Automate?

In the light of what we discussed in Chapter 1, you might believe that business leaders would be falling over themselves to automate as many processes as they possibly can, while keeping a keen eye out for opportunities to implement more technology as time goes by. It's not so, and given what we now know about the capabilities of software, the reason for this is somewhat ironic.

I've spoken to countless executives and entrepreneurs during my career, and I hear the same statement repeatedly. It goes something like this:

'I know we should be doing that. We'd love to automate, but we're bogged down in the admin and must do that before we can do the important stuff.'

The trap of busywork is familiar and alluring. The business demands our full attention, pulling us into a vortex of customer requests, documentation, administration, deliverables, team and management tasks. Even in established businesses, leaders can succumb to this trap. The urgency to work *in* the company overshadows the need to work *on* the company, making it a survival imperative rather than a strategic choice.

As businesses grow, they often employ more staff to handle increasing workloads. The problem I've found is that, often, companies develop specific ways of working over time, creating processes that become deeply ingrained in their operations. These established procedures are often followed without question, even when they're no longer efficient. As a result, businesses continue to perform certain tasks manually or inefficiently, when, with the right software solutions, these processes could be automated or streamlined.

It's both frustrating and exciting for me to see this in action. Companies don't invest the time to implement new systems to improve certain processes because these processes, however inefficient, are ingrained and producing results. Companies may not even consider investing in a software system that will automate the processes, as they're focused on maintaining current operations rather than innovating for growth. Decision makers might not realise how inefficient these processes are, know how to improve them or understand that significant improvements are possible.

This observation is coming from a place of deep empathy, not judgement. Many businesses get caught in this trap for years until they finally spot it and take steps to change the situation; the results can be phenomenal and life-changing. The excitement is that when I see an organisation caught in this trap, I know that there's an opportunity for its leaders to make a huge impact on their operations and overall business performance.

If it feels like your company may be in this trap, what you need are systems and processes. A set of supportive systems can free both you and your team members from the repetitive and dull tasks that are taking up time you and they could be using to add huge amounts of value to the business and the world. Comprehensive processes mean that anyone who needs to do a task can do it in the same way *each time,* exactly as you intended.

Taking a step back and seeing this is such an important and game-changing activity. When my team and I run our Clarity Workshops and investigate how much time teams are spending on work that could be automated, we find it tends to be a large amount of their day. This is not only unnecessary, it's a massive drawback for the company.

Superpowers

I tend to use a superhero analogy to describe the business admin trap – I like superheroes! How would the DC Universe and the City of Metropolis fare if Clark

Kent was too busy writing for *The Daily Planet* to save the world as Superman? Can you imagine?

'I've got an article deadline, I need to finish my investigative story on the corruption of suburban estate agents.'

That is probably important to a niche readership, Clark, but is there a chance that Lois Lane could work on the story while you show the S on your chest and fly off to prevent Lex Luthor from destroying the city?

With processes in place, Lois knows exactly when and how to write that article, and to submit it to the editor on time. What's more, Lois is a great journalist; frankly, much better than Clark. The final product would be submitted on time, be of better quality, and Superman would have saved the world again. It's a no brainer, right?

Let's bring this analogy into the real world. With a process in place for submitting, say, a blog article to a medium publication, our modern-day Lois Lane could simply write the article and send it to her assistant or virtual assistant (VA). They can then follow Lois's processes for copyrighting, meta data and article submission. This way, Lois is free to focus on her superpower too – to write and report – rather than being bogged down by the details of submission. She can even use AI to help her outline and draft the story up front so that her time is spent where the real value is – word craft.

CASE STUDY

At Remote, we've designed a system to make our support process as smooth as possible. Our delivery manager keeps an eye on our customer support portal, ensuring prompt action on incoming support tickets. When a ticket comes in, she reaches out to the client to gather all the necessary details about the issue. With this information, she creates a ticket on our Kanban board and informs our scrum master, who manages the board. Together, they assess the task's priority level.

The ticket is then positioned correctly on the board, so that the appropriate member of our development team can pick it up at the right time. This approach ensures that our support process seamlessly integrates with our development process, which operates as its own structured sequence. (Later in the book, we'll explore how various processes within a business overlap and interlink.)

Once the support issue is resolved, the ticket status on the Kanban board is updated to 'resolved'. Our delivery manager then checks in with the client to confirm that the issue has been fixed, ensuring clear communication and client satisfaction.

Processes like these can be kept simple for ease of repetition, but can also incorporate layers of complexity and decision making. There are so many tasks my team does every day that benefit from systems and processes, which provide real leverage. The degree to which you can automate your processes is the degree to which you can experience exponential growth in your business.

After identifying each team member's values and unique strengths – their superpowers – you can understand their role within the team. You then delegate or automate tasks that don't align with these strengths or values, ensuring that each person is focused on what they do best.

Software systems have become a cornerstone of every successful business, improving productivity and efficiency, and lowering overheads, but now, we all have the chance to move into a new era of supportive systems. These are designed around a company's values, the roles of its team members and their individual strengths, filling gaps where necessary, supporting each team member within their key role. They integrate the alignment of values and purpose across individuals, teams and the organisation into every process, keeping everyone on track with personal and organisational goals while lightening their workload.

This allows team members to leverage their unique strengths more often. Through intelligent reporting, everyone can understand not only what they're doing and how effectively they're doing it, but also why they're doing it and the impact it has on the organisation. The disconnect between the cog and the machine is removed, and team members feel a full sense of worth and empowerment. When the systems are correctly aligning work with meaning, impact and purpose, the organisation can produce exponential growth and make a real difference, adding genuine value to its customers as well as its team members. Profit is an inevitable side-effect of such a system.

As entrepreneur and best-selling author Daniel Priestley says in his essential book *24 Assets* (2017):

> 'A 200-tonne plane takes off in flight because it was designed to; the pilot doesn't need a pep-talk to get it airborne. A Porsche 911 accelerates swiftly to 100km/h because of the engineering; the passenger seat isn't put there for a guru to stir the driver up. A 100-storey building stays upright in a storm because of its architecture and construction; it doesn't require motivational quotes to reinforce its structure.'

A business is the emergent property of its systems. Get the systems right and continue to improve them, adding more where you see a gap, and the emergent business is reliable, sustainable, profitable and a joy to be part of.

Let's dive into the world of systems and processes to see how we can reveal that S on your chest and enhance the superpowers of your team at the same time.

Visualising automation

While I talk about automation in the context of this book, I recognise that there are many other types, from AI-driven agriculture making farming more effective, efficient and sustainable, to robotics transforming the world of manufacturing. Even the self-checkouts that are now ubiquitous in our supermarkets are a type of automation. Here, I'm concerned with using software to manage our business operations, automating processes where possible and facilitating more intuitive workflows where human interaction is necessary.

You're likely already using some software automation, even if it's only in small ways. Have you ever set an email autoresponder when you go on holiday? That's a basic example – software carrying out a task for you to simplify your life.

Now let's expand that concept. What if the same technology could provide weekly progress reports to a client or deliver a training programme through a series of emails and videos? It could streamline customer or employee onboarding. Imagine an accessible customer portal where orders can be placed, modified and tracked at any time.

Let's take the legal profession as an example. Much of this profession revolves around document management – conducting searches, compiling certificates, contracts and more. Imagine a software system capable of collecting necessary details from a client, executing searches via application programming interfaces (APIs) and generating contracts. These contracts could then be forwarded to a third-party lawyer for online signature and comments, freeing up the original solicitor for other tasks. With this approach, document or contract errors are significantly reduced, and the process can be repeated endlessly with minimal lawyer interaction.

Using software, you can obtain, onboard and look after new customers, with relevant documents, tutorials, guides and reports sent to them with no outside interference from a human member of the team. Consistently high quality, on time, to the right person, in the right format. Orders taken, processed and sent to a warehouse stock picker in moments. Entire services delivered via an online portal, connecting supplier directly with consumer. Comprehensive inventory management, re-ordering, reporting at a multi-warehouse scale. Performance management, financial forecasting. All done by software that's set up once and left to work, while you get on with building customer relationships, innovating new product lines, creating joint-venture partnerships, and anything else that aligns with your own interests, values and natural talents.

Once you've looked at your existing business processes and automated and systemised those, your profit margins will be higher and your stress levels lower. You'll spend a lot less time managing the day-to-day admin, and your team will work with more momentum, more flow and less guidance from managers or you.

That means that you're free to work on the next stage of the automation process: the innovation. Once you've taken existing processes and either made them simpler to perform or automated them completely using software, you can start looking at brand new ways to deliver your products and services. This usually means creating products and services that can be delivered digitally via an online or mobile application. Rethinking your industry means questioning long-standing norms and embodying disruption. It's about revolutionising how your industry operates using cutting-edge technology and innovative ideas. Think of Uber transforming the private vehicle hire industry; Airbnb reimagining holiday rentals and bed and breakfast markets; LinkedIn and PayPal reshaping business networking and online payments respectively.

The great thing about disruption is that we don't need to have multi-million-dollar budgets to pull it off. The huge, dominant players listed above started from scratch. Their enormous growth and substantial revenues resulted from their courage to challenge their industry norms early on. They dared to be different, and they transformed into titans.

Powerful ideas are often quite simple ones. What's difficult is having the courage to come up with an idea that we know, if it works, will cause disruption to our own industry, change the way that we do business and maybe even put our existing company out of business altogether. This is the challenge and the opportunity for those of us who choose to step up to the frontline: we must burn down the forest to allow the new shoots to grow, and that can be scary to those of us who have spent years cultivating that forest. Even those who are ready and willing to do so can be too bogged down in the admin of their current way of working to make the headspace to innovate.

There's our opportunity: not everyone is up to the task of disrupting and automating. It's too much of a challenge to the status quo and it requires time and energy, but those who don't will be disrupted by those who do. We must risk burning down our own forest so that we can be part of the new one.

When to automate

There's a good chance you know what it looks like when the systems in a business fail to meet the demands that are placed on them. Communication breaks down; customers constantly call to chase work or products; sales drop; reputations are damaged. You need to hire more people to meet demand, fill gaps or bring in work, yet with every new hire, the levels of complexity go up. You create more lines of communication, need more management, more meetings, get less actual work done and profit margins continue to fall.

Your business strategy pendulums from 'bring in more sales' to 'build more capacity'. This is a natural part of business, but software systems can act like car suspension on a bumpy road, smoothing out the knocks and allowing you to turn on the tap of sales, manage more clients and turn around more work, keeping you in control of the business, rather than the other way round.

The problem we have is that we all tend to think about our systems at the point when those systems are already failing. What got us to this point is suddenly not enough, and we find ourselves in reactive rather than proactive mode. When we become reactive, our ability to work intentionally is removed and we lose sovereignty over our actions and strategy. Work priorities fall into the *urgent* column, demanding our attention now, and so our view of the horizon and our ability to navigate to where we want to get to is lost.

Once we're in that position, we'll find ourselves in an ever-decreasing circle of defence. There's no time to consider and act on long-term strategy. No time, headspace or funds to invest in the systems that will get us out of the situation and back on track towards our goals. The only option is to limp along with the systems that got us this far and ride a plateau.

Plateaus become dips way sooner than we may expect. To build is to grow. To grow is to thrive.

The ideal is to stay in strategy mode. To plan your moves ahead of time and set your goals, navigating your way towards them confidently and with strength. From this mode, you're proactive, you've got mojo, you're walking with a swagger.

Anticipate potential bottlenecks and develop software solutions to prevent them from constraining your growth before you need them. When a business launches, a mix of off-the-shelf systems like Monday, Airtable or Trello for operations, ActiveCampaign or HubSpot for customer relationship management (CRM), and a WordPress website for sales often suffices. Zapier (pronounced 'Happier') keeps a rough data integrity between them and everything is fine, but as teams expand, these systems can start to show their limits.

Often, around the £5m revenue mark or a twenty-member team, businesses begin to experience the strain of the systems that got them there. Employees find themselves repetitively copying and pasting between software or creating additional spreadsheets to compensate for features that aren't provided by their current systems.

A red flag at this stage is when most operational knowledge sits in the head of the longest-serving employee. The mounting pressure from their workload, memory demands and constant questions means they could leave at any minute, taking all their accumulated knowledge and company IP with them.

When we're in offence rather than defence mode as business leaders, we call the shots, and we do this by designing and building our systems before we need them; building for where we are, but also where we're heading. Doing this takes us to our goals more quickly, helps us keep our margins high and lets us invest in technology when we have the finances and headspace to do it, rather than when we're stressed out, stuck in busywork and dangerously low on profit margins.

3
Overcoming Resistance

You now know why you must have automation systems and processes in place appropriate to both where your business is and where it's going, but you might still encounter resistance when implementing these systems. The most frustrating thing about this resistance is that it often comes from you as the business leader.

Why is this? There are four big reasons why organisational leaders resist putting in place systems and processes:

1. Time investment

2. Financial investment

3. Not knowing where to start

4. Fear of change

In this chapter, we'll look at each one in turn.

Time investment

It's a situation we all tend to know too well. We have work to do and the pressure of a looming deadline. The goal is to just get the task finished; there's no room to note down a step-by-step guide for someone to follow in the future. Deep down, we suspect this entire task could be automated, freeing up precious time down the line, but the prospect of setting up systems and dealing with the learning curve pushes us away. Instead, we focus, keep our heads down and complete the task at hand.

Let's face it: this is a common scenario that everyone in business can relate to. When our to-do list seems to stretch indefinitely, the last thing we want is for a task to take longer than usual, even if the extra work promises to save time in the future. It's a psychological tug-of-war. We convince ourselves we're close to conquering that mammoth backlog that's been hanging over us. Soon, we think, our schedule will clear, and we'll have time to set up automated systems and document our processes, but that time is not now, not this week.

Perhaps this thought process strikes a chord with you. If so, you'll be aware that the elusive 'free week in the near future' never arrives. It's a perpetually shifting timeframe as you continuously slot new tasks into the openings in your upcoming schedule.

This imagined utopia, where no deadlines or urgent tasks demand our attention, will always remain out of reach. As a result, the investment of time we need to establish systems and processes, which we know will pay dividends later, only gets attention once our workload has already ballooned. It's at this stage we're fighting to stay afloat, unable to scale, in disarray and urgently in need of those systems and processes to salvage the situation.

Wouldn't it be better to set everything up ahead of time, before we're under pressure and short on hours? To realise that software systems might prevent us from descending into chaos by ensuring that we stay on top of things with enough time to manage our tasks efficiently?

Establish automated systems so software can handle tasks like sending invoice reminders, keeping customers informed, distributing work items to your team and processing purchase orders. Let technology run your operations, allowing you to focus on the tasks that matter; the tasks unique to your skillset; the tasks that align with your superpower.

Any time spent outside of those skillsets is a waste, as you can create 10x more impact when you are doing the things that no one else in your business can do. I'd go so far as to say that any time spent outside of your unique skillset should be considered a failure of your systems. Time invested in building the correct systems places you back in the driver's seat of your career and your business, doing the work you were born to do.

Financial investment

The struggle here is equally understandable, and equally important to address. Setting up systems and processes inevitably requires some kind of financial investment, whether it's paying for custom software to be built, subscribing to an online service or even paying your team or a VA to spend time setting the systems up when they could be doing work that directly earns money for the organisation. It can feel scary to invest money in something that you can't immediately see will bring an improvement on revenue, which, traditionally and historically in business, has been the only thing that matters.

As a business leader, you may well be submerged in operational tasks. Answering emails, scheduling appointments, sorting bills, managing projects, writing proposals, producing content – it feels endless.

What happens when you outsource these tasks? By paying someone £20 per hour to take on some of these jobs, you free up a significant amount of time in your schedule. You can spend that time on tasks that sit squarely in your wheelhouse, so your value per hour can skyrocket. How much can you earn when you're working on the thing you're best at? Perhaps

£250–£300 per hour? More? By spending that £20 per hour, you can save yourself time that could be exponentially more valuable.

Translate that to software. If custom software frees up twenty hours per week that you can now spend on your superpower tasks, the financial impact can be profound. For instance, if this focused work brings in £300 per hour, freeing up 20 hours translates to an additional £6,000 per week, or £312,000 per year. What happens when you apply the concept to a team or across your entire operation? When you invest in custom software, the investment can sometimes be substantial, but the returns can be huge.

And there's another factor to consider: energy. It's exhausting to work on tasks that don't align with your strengths. The constant context switching can be mentally taxing. Imagine instead focusing your efforts on the high-value tasks, working within a single sustained energy stream. The potential returns could be extraordinary, proving the importance of rhythm and flow in business.

In the previous chapter, I talked about the £5m in revenue or twenty staff-member threshold. At this point, it's difficult to continue to provide quality and value to your customers, and even more difficult to continue to scale gracefully. If automated systems could increase revenue by only 2%, you'd be looking at £100,000 return in the first year. That's a £half-million return in five years. Would it be worth a £150,000 investment over that time to generate that return?

I love the way Daniel Priestley puts this in an interview with the *Strike It Big* podcast (Tilbury and Priestley, 2024):

'Imagine you had a box, and whenever you put £7,000 in, £35,000 came out in ten days. How much would you put in the box?'

CASE STUDY

At Remote, we once built a software system to streamline a manual process for an international client. Originally, the client's yearly expense for this process hovered around £30k. Deciding to invest in technology, they spent £90k on our software solution. The results were impressive.

In just the first year, the accuracy improvement of our system compared to the manual process saved the client's business more than £20m. That's not a typo. Over £20m saved in just a year.

Fast forward a decade and they're still using the system. Not only has it saved them the £300k that would've been spent on the manual process, but the continual accuracy enhancements of the software have also led to ongoing savings in the millions.

This case illustrates how, when you have clear outcomes and can pinpoint prime areas for automation, investing in the right systems can bring incredible returns. It's a powerful testament to the potential of purpose-built software.

Finally, remember that reducing the time it takes to deliver your product isn't just reducing the cost of creating the product. It's freeing up time to turn around more products with the same resources – that's a direct increase in revenue.

We'll talk in more detail about how to calculate the potential ROI of a custom software development in Part Two. In the meantime, if you're keen to do some exploration yourself, you can use my free ROI calculator in the online resources I've created for this book.

Visit https://paulmcgillivray.com/resources to get started.

Not knowing where to start

You now know that investing the time to implement automated systems will save much more time in the future. You know that investing the money will both save and make money in the future. You know that your processes can be automated, streamlined, delegated, improved. However, the problem of where to start can be overwhelming and a source of frustration and, inevitably, procrastination.

Part Two of this book is dedicated to walking you through the steps you need to follow to embrace automation. Take it step by step, task by task, process by process, and it's straightforward and simple to amplify your impact exponentially.

When you work according to the SCOPE framework, checking both your aims and assumptions along the way, you always know the next step. Each step is geared to inform the next while giving you the confidence to move forward in the knowledge that you're levelling up yourself and your business.

Fear of change

This is something else that's so common in business, I'm sure you've encountered it before. As humans, we are hardwired to resist change (Pennington, 2018). It's an evolutionary thing: our brain views change as a threat, so puts us into fight or flight mode. This was great for our distant ancestors who could interpret a change in their surroundings correctly and be focused and ready to leap into action before a sabre-toothed tiger could leap on them. It's not so great in our modern business world where change is the new normal, and we have to keep up or we will rapidly be left behind.

This means that now, rather that reacting in fight or flight mode, where we're not capable of any kind of measured thought beyond dealing with the perceived threat, we need to train ourselves and our employees to meet change head on and embrace it. As with anything that involves pushing ourselves outside of our comfort zone, the best way to get good at this is to practise. What feels horribly uncomfortable at first soon becomes habit as our comfort zone expands to encapsulate change.

This is the only way to grow as business leaders, and thereby to grow our businesses. Change is not our enemy, it's our friend. Welcome it into your life as such, starting with the multitude of positive changes that automation can bring about, the most pertinent of which we have covered in this chapter.

Reading on from here is an investment in your liberation. I want you to finish this book with confidence in where to start automating your systems and processes, what to expect and how to go about it. You'll know how to identify the part of your business where software will give you the biggest ROI in momentum, resources and time. You'll know what to look for in a development partner. You'll know how to make sure you build the right thing and that your new software integrates smoothly into your existing business operations. You'll know how to measure its success and adjust as necessary for maximum impact. You'll know how to navigate the process of custom software development with ease, avoiding common pitfalls and misconceptions. You'll know how to effectively communicate your needs and expectations to a development team, ensuring your vision is realised.

Your journey to software-driven success starts here. The power to revolutionise your business operations, increase your efficiency and boost your profits is in your hands. Part Two will equip you with not only the knowledge, but also the confidence to take that first step towards transforming your business through custom software. It will walk you through how to identify the bottlenecks and opportunities using the methods the Remote team runs in our Clarity Work-shops, but before you begin, our scorecard will give you a good sense right away of where you are.

Visit https://paulmcgillivray.com/resources or scan the QR code to access the scorecard and the other resources I've made available for free for you.

Once you've done that, take a deep breath, turn the page and let's begin this adventure together. You're not just reading a book – you're taking the first step towards a more efficient, profitable and satisfying future for your business.

Let's turn potential into reality. Let's make it happen.

PART TWO
THE SCOPE FRAMEWORK

4

Strategise

To build a business takes grit, determination and resilience. To scale it takes courage and intelligence. It requires smart thinking.

You can't graft your way to scale. Keep on pushing for too long, you're likely to burn out and give up. Scaling takes more than the incremental improvements that graft can bring you. You need to work smarter, not harder, and that takes the kind of 10x thinking that software can excel at implementing.

If you aim to do something 10% better, with hard work and grit, you can probably succeed. To do that thing 10x better, you need to completely rethink the way you do it to achieve anything close to that goal.

Imagine you've been challenged to outperform your current metrics in your business. Aiming for a 10% improvement might lead you to renegotiate supplier contracts or upgrade to faster servers – both valuable but incremental changes. Now consider the bigger goal of 10x improvement.

Suddenly you're looking at a complete overhaul of your supply chain rather than just renegotiating contracts. You're not hiring a bit more efficiently by streamlining the interview process, you're throwing open the doors to a global talent pool by embracing remote work. You're not squeezing a bit more out of your advertising budget; you're creating a viral brand campaign that turns your customers into your most potent marketers.

You're not just improving, you're transforming.

This isn't about working harder on your existing path; 10x thinking is about finding an entirely new path that catapults you towards your goal. Right now in business, software is that path. Software built for your business. From inception, with scale as its purpose.

No matter what your business does, if it's not driven by software, the chances are you're going to be beaten by a competitor that has found a way to use software to leverage their offering. I can't stress enough how important this point is. It's the whole reason I've written this book. I need you to understand what software can do for you, how to put it in place and how imperative it is for you to do that before it's too late. After working with many businesses in this position over the years, I sense the urgency of this viscerally.

In Part One, we've talked about what software automation can do and what the implications may be of ignoring the technology tide. You now need to step up and implement software systems in the key areas of your business that will provide you with that 10x lift.

Part Two will guide you through the process so that you know how to find the parts of the business under strain, and how to turn them into the most profit-making and successful departments. You'll be empowered to work with a development team to do this, because you'll know what they should be doing and what the deliverables should look like. You'll know what to expect and when, and as a result, you'll recognise red flags early, so you can keep this project on track, to budget and achieving its objectives.

To do this, you're going to follow the method my team and I have developed at Remote. The SCOPE framework has evolved over our years of working on projects and iterating our processes. Putting various tried and trusted methods together with ones we've developed ourselves and adding our unique Remote spice, we came up with our own take on successful application development.

SCOPE takes the best elements of user experience (UX) design and business analysis, innovation principles and world-class delivery processes, and multiplies their effect with powerful iterative transformation. The five steps are:

1. **Strategise** – work out where you want to go

2. **Clarify** – get clear on where you're at now

3. **Optimise** – work out how you're going to get to your goals

4. **Prototype** – test your assumptions early

5. **Execute** – deliver and iterate

As we progress through the sections of the framework, you'll gain insights into what should happen at each point, with things to do and avoid, along with advice on how to implement your ideas. Each step is essential.

It can be tempting to just dive in and get going with the whole thing – you're a visionary, you see the entire five-year plan already, right? Diving in and building everything you can think of up-front is not a wise decision. If you skip any part of this framework, you could be signing up for a bumpy ride. Taking your development in small steps, testing with your team and your customers along the way, is a safer, more enjoyable and faster way to achieve your goals.

I'll show you how with the SCOPE methodology. Follow it right, and you'll be riding the wave of success and achieving things in your business you didn't dare dream of.

Step One of SCOPE

Now you know what to expect, let's get started on Step One: Strategise.

I remember the first time I recognised that automation is advancing fast and changing everything in its wake. The irony was that I'd been evangelising about the emergence of tech for some time – as I run a software company, it's pretty much a default conversation topic.

A naive part of me had discounted the fact that no industry is immune to the advancement and disruption of tech, not even the software industry. All at once, I saw the wave of new tech and innovation that was emerging in my industry, and what it was about to do to the business I'd been running for eighteen years. I felt a sense of urgency, maybe even panic.

I handled it badly. Rushing into Remote's open-plan office, I began rambling to my team about how everything's going to change and we need to relook at how we do business. I still remember the confused and astonished looks on everyone's faces!

Learn from my mistakes here. Confusion and panic are not the best responses to this realisation. You need to respond, absolutely, but first work out where you're at and where you need to be.

Forming a good strategy at this point will facilitate a more powerful, pragmatic and positive transformation. The last thing you need is to make a rash decision and spend the next few months or years implementing the wrong thing because you're unclear on your objectives.

Address and avoid this danger with the Strategise step of the framework. You'll get clear on where you are now, where you're going and what could be improved, what to do about it, and in what order to execute your plan. Then you can move forward.

CASE STUDY

A client in the rapid manufacturing industry approached us at a growth milestone: £5m turnover with a team of twenty. They managed operations with Microsoft Access and Excel, relying heavily on a single administrator – a significant vulnerability.

During two Clarity Workshops, we discovered that their processes had evolved organically, leading to administrative overhead and time-consuming data processing. Key issues included:

- **Duplication of data:** Manually entering the same data into multiple spreadsheets
- **Lack of customisable reporting:** Inability to generate specific reports
- **No standardised quality reviews:** Inconsistent quality control across locations
- **Inconsistent processes:** Different practices due to too many free text fields.

Our Strategise process identified several impactful software solutions:

- **Centralised data model:** We moved all data to a cloud-based system for consistency and accessibility.
- **Automated workflow:** We created a light-touch workflow that required less administrative intervention.

- **'Sleep at night' dashboard:** We developed a dashboard for key metrics.

- **Request for quote (RFQ) system:** We implemented a new RFQ process through which customers could log in, fill out RFQs and upload CAD drawings. The system notified relevant team members and tracked RFQ status, reducing delays and errors.

- **Automated quote management:** This allowed suppliers to upload quotes, which the system used to calculate margins and generate customer quotes, speeding up the process.

- **Purchase order integration:** This enabled automatic generation of purchase orders and status updates across platforms, reducing manual entry and errors.

This illustrates the effectiveness of our Strategise process in identifying bottlenecks and inefficiencies. By designing a centralised system, we improved communication between customers, suppliers and the core team, significantly reducing the time taken to manage each step in the order and delivery process.

Any time you save by not planning thoroughly will be lost over and over by you implementing the wrong solution that doesn't address the right points or, worse, doesn't work at all and must be scrapped.

At Remote, we've had many clients come to us having worked with a software company that's poorly implemented the planning stage and had to abandon the project tens of thousands of pounds in. Why? Either unexpected needs emerged, and the software's design just couldn't keep up, or the company built something that wasn't what the client needed in the first place. In other words, they weren't straight on the strategy before they started.

It's like being halfway through a building construction job and discovering that the architect hasn't put a supporting wall in a place that needs to bear a heavy load. If it was in the drawings at the start, it would have been no problem at all. With two floors already up, there's no chance.

Skipping the Strategise stage is a key reason why software projects fail. Other reasons include:

- **Poor requirements analysis**. Misunderstanding needs leads to software that misses the mark.

- **Communication breakdown**. When stakeholders fail to connect, errors sneak in.

- **Superficial testing**. Without thorough checks, critical bugs slip through.

- **Resource drought**. Time, budget, talent – any shortage can stall a project.

- **Project mismanagement**. Poor planning, coordination and control can throw a project off track.

- **Technical debt**. Rushed delivery can lead to slow, unmanageable software.

- **Dismissed user feedback**. Ignoring the end users can turn a potentially good product into a failure.

- **Outpaced by technology**. In the tech world, change is constant. Fall behind and you risk becoming obsolete.

- **Risk ignorance**. Overlooking risks today can cause project failures tomorrow.

Strategise is the foundation that works to prevent these problems – failing to plan is planning to fail. It begins by getting a wide-angle overview of your business.

The destination defines the journey

To determine a path between where you are now and where you're heading, you need to get clear on your destination. It might sound obvious, but it's surprising how many business leaders implement software without a definition of success or a target to aim for.

The main reason for this is that they tend to take a *technology first* approach to software implementation: 'We have this software tool, what can we use it for?'

Instead, we should take a *purpose first* approach: 'We need to achieve x; how can technology help us?'

When you have a target, the obstacles to that target become clear. The absence of a destination creates a plateau, which inevitably leads to a downward spiral. When you add more momentum to a downward spiral, you simply hit the bottom more quickly.

Think about what metrics are important to you and would serve as indicators of progress towards your vision. Here are some key metrics to keep in mind as you go through the process in this book.

Growth

Growth is the pulse of a business; when we talk about scale, we're usually referring to growth. You can measure it in several ways, so pick the metrics that are most indicative of success in your business. Popular key performance indicators (KPIs) are annual revenue, number of customers, amount of profit or revenue per employee. Customer and staff churn are also indicative metrics.

Pick what works for your business and choose a set of target numbers that, when hit, will let you know you've achieved your goals.

Financial performance

Although I've mentioned financial metrics above, they'll be monitoring the growth of the business. Financial health is another thing altogether; you can have high revenue but terrible cash flow, for example. Also consider looking at metrics like ROI (how much money you receive back for every pound you spend on the business), debtor days (how long it takes for your business to get paid) and debt-to-equity ratio.

Once you have your numbers, put them on a dashboard, make them visible and refer to them regularly. Ensure that the decisions you make and the assumptions you write down later in the process are directly aimed at moving these numbers closer to your goals. They'll be your compass as you continue your transformational journey.

The Pareto principle

The last metric we'll consider here is one that I've regularly seen have profound effects on business in a positive way. Designed by economist Vilfredo Pareto in the nineteenth century, the Pareto principle or 80/20 rule appears to apply to almost everything in nature, but in business, there are two applications of it that can be game changing:

1. 20% of your clients bring in 80% of your profits. Conversely, 80% of your clients bring in 20% of your profits.

2. 20% of the work that you and each member of your team do brings in 80% of the impact/ income. Conversely, 80% of your work brings in only 20% of your income.

We need to keep our focus on those profitable 20% of clients, and ourselves and our team constantly working within the 20% that has the 80% impact. Either dropping the 80% of clients that bring in the 20% or using software to manage them for us can lead to huge ROI alongside higher profits, motivation, momentum and impact.

The 20% of work that generates 80% of the impact is where we truly excel. This is the work that puts us in a state of flow, leveraging our unique skills and strengths – our superpowers. (Remember our Clark Kent/Superman analogy in Part One?) When we focus on these tasks, we create momentum and achieve remarkable results. Our goal should be to maximise the time each team member spends on these high-impact activities. By doing so, we not only enhance productivity and motivation, but also drive substantial growth and success for the business. When you decide which processes to apply software support to first, add the 80/20 principle to your decision making for maximum effect.

Understanding your business landscape

Perspective is everything. To see what's going on in our business in a holistic and useful way, we need to step back and look at the big picture.

This act of stepping back can be a difficult one, even if it's a very small concern. We are so involved in the business for most of the time, we don't have a clear view of what's going on at any given moment, and cause and effect can be hard to see, even if we've been carrying out the same processes and delivering the same products or services for years. In fact, it can be much harder in that case, because we do so many things without thinking, we often don't notice that we are doing them.

To really understand how to improve your business processes and operations, you need to adopt a big-picture view. Only then will you see your business with fresh eyes and spot the things that are causing frustration, or could be causing delight.

How? There are a few proven methods and I'll share a couple with you now, so you'll be able to see your business and the way it operates in a whole new light. First, it's a deep dive into the wonder of systems thinking, devised in the 1950s by Professor Jay Forrester (Lutkevich, 2007).

Systems thinking

A system is a group of items that interact with each other to perform a particular purpose or function. Two wheels, a chain, a cog, a seat, a frame and handlebars are separate parts, but together form a bicycle. Changing the size of the wheels or the ratio of the cog to the chain affects the bike's performance. A bicycle is a single thing on its own, but only because that is what we call that particular group of interdependent parts. That's a system.

We can zoom in to any part of the bicycle – say, the wheel – and see that it is a system made up of a rubber tyre, spokes, ball bearings etc. Changing the type of rubber for the tyre or the air pressure inside it will affect the performance of the wheel and the bike.

If you get on your bike and ride it into town, you become part of the traffic system. Interact by buying a coffee and you affect the town's economic system. You will also affect other connected systems as you continue to interact with the town, such as the social system, the community, ecological systems, families and culture.

Zoom out some more and you see multiple towns and cities affecting each other and joining together to become a national system – otherwise known as a country. Of course, you can continue to zoom out and see the countries interacting with each other, affected by weather systems and global economic systems. Zoom out again and you see planetary systems and even galaxies interacting and influencing each other.

The most minute of actions can cause a dramatic domino effect of subsequent actions, leading to a seemingly unrelated result. Your decision to get on your bike and head into town changes the workings of 1,000 systems, which may affect systems you know nothing about, perhaps even years into the future.

When considering systems, an interesting and perhaps vital definition to make upfront is that if you have a collection of parts that aren't interdependent or interacting together for a specific purpose, then what you have is a collection of parts or objects, not a system. A good test to discover which one you have is to remove one part – if the others still function and continue to work towards their purpose, then you didn't have a system, you had a collection.

For example, if I took the wheel off the bike I described earlier, it wouldn't continue to function in the same way. If I removed a pen from a stationery cupboard, it would remain a stationery cupboard – because the stationery is a collection, not a system.

Analysis is the study of the individual parts of a system. Science is particularly good at this. Each part is studied independently – cells of the body, a particular organ or a type of gas in the atmosphere. Systems thinking looks at these things holistically.

The system we're interested in here is your business. In systems thinking terms, your business has a required output (your product or service). It processes various inputs to achieve that output (finances, a brief or product order, human resources etc). If you can get a view of the various parts and systems that comprise your business, then you can understand what levers to push and pull to improve its output.

Put simply, understanding and improving your business's internal processes can boost its overall performance. A business is a complex network of internal systems, all interconnecting and interacting. The quality of its output hinges on how well these systems work together.

A business might thrive thanks to a strong team culture, efficient processes or effective management, but that's not the whole picture. External factors such as the state of the economy, industry trends or the availability of skilled workers locally can also play significant roles. These external factors are in turn influenced by a wide array of economic and environmental elements.

The big takeaway here is that business doesn't exist in a vacuum. It's part of a much larger and more intricate system.

Our task here is to recognise the parts of our system we *can* change while allowing for movement and pressures from those that we *can't*. We must also do our best to recognise the effect those changes will have on other parts of our system so that improving one thing doesn't have a detrimental influence on something else. At the same time, we realise that even the smallest changes to the parts can reap huge benefits to the overall system, just like shifting gears on the bike moves the chain on to a disc only a couple of centimetres different in size to the one it had been on, but the improved performance the cyclist gets at the right time is massive.

The key to profits, to scale without frustration, to high performance and to a thriving culture is operational efficiency. It's about how effectively our business system works. Fine-tune the operations, and the results in other parts of our business improve exponentially.

Systems thinking gives us the perspective we need to analyse and understand the interaction of our business as a system. By looking at the whole system rather than only its parts, we can get a clearer view of what's happening and what could be improved. We can then focus on the smaller systems or processes within it that need changing or improving.

Essentially, every system consists of three interactions:

1. **Reinforcing loop:** With this kind of loop, the effect of a change compounds, creating momentum. This momentum can happen in either a good or a bad direction.

2. **Balancing loop:** This happens to bring something under control and in line with where it should be.

3. **Threshold:** This is the point at which the action meets a trigger point, causing a different action.

I'm going to use everyday examples to show what each interaction means. Let's use a simple one to start: the restaurant.

If one restaurant is empty and another on the opposite side of the street has plenty of people in it, all being equal, the number of people in each restaurant will act as a reinforcing loop. Passers-by will assume that the restaurant with more customers in it is the better one, and so will go inside – meaning that the condition of both restaurants is reinforced. The empty one stays empty, and the full one gets fuller. Queues outside restaurants lead to bigger queues outside restaurants.

Balancing happens at two points. If a restaurant gets so full that waiting times are longer than customers are prepared to tolerate, they'll stop queuing for a table. That point is referred to as the threshold. Hit that threshold and balancing occurs – customers leave the queue, which diminishes.

If the empty restaurant needs more customers, it'll employ various tactics: a new chef, interesting menus, signs outside, efficient processes, better food, building reputation and so on. Those tactics act as a balance and attract more people to the restaurant.

In both cases, balancing sets momentum in the opposite direction to which it was previously going. We can see this in every type of system – the sense of feeling hungry or full acts as a balancing loop in our body. We stop eating when we hit a threshold of either food available or our body's requirement for that food. A bicycle gets faster or slower depending on the momentum that drives it – it has thresholds for how fast or slow it's possible to go. The value of an individual's stocks and shares goes up or down depending on whether those stocks and shares are already going up or down. The intrinsic value of the stocks acts as a balancing loop for the stock's value, making corrections if hype, news or trend sets the values on a reinforcing loop for too long.

The systems we build will affect the momentum of work in our business. A business with many customers is seen as in demand, and therefore wins more customers. A business desperate for work is seen as such and has trouble winning customers.

Your business is made up of a series of interacting systems that affect each other, with reinforcing and balancing loops hitting thresholds constantly, while being hit by the effects of outside systems, too. Business strategy of all kinds essentially boils down to the art of recognising and using these loops and thresholds to your advantage, reducing or reversing the negative loops and enhancing the positive ones.

These interactions work all the way down to the granular level; workload, logistics, morale all play a part in your business, and the way that one works will often affect the others. Your eventual aim is to spot these loops and thresholds in your business and manage them using software for optimum performance.

We're going to build on systems thinking as we move on to our next section, the Theory of Constraints (TOC). These two concepts combined will inform your work as you carry out the Strategise stage of SCOPE so that you improve the most important parts of your operations first and don't accidentally create a feedback loop that makes things worse rather than better.

Theory of Constraints

One of the first business books I ever read was, by chance, also one of the most influential. *The Goal* by Eliyahu M Goldratt is a powerful business management tool written in the form of a fictional novel (1984).

In the book, Goldratt introduces his TOC. A deep understanding and implementation of this has informed and improved my team's work at Remote for over twenty years, and it is a key principle for you to understand so that you too can analyse and design your business process systems. I recommend that you read the full book, and the others on the same theme by Goldratt, especially the sequel, *It's Not Luck* (2002), but I'll summarise here in a way that puts his work in the context of what we need to achieve with our software.

The TOC was conceived for the manufacturing industry, but just as we business leaders have done with the Lean manufacturing process (Landau, 2023) and countless others, we can easily transfer it over to the software design sector – and, in fact, any business sector. Every business system (as I'm sure you'll remember from the previous section, every business *is* a system) comprises a series of events. Each event depends on a previous event to be completed before it can be addressed.

For example, if you run a courier company, you can't deliver a parcel before you've received it into your depot, and you can't receive it before it's been collected from a pickup point, and it can't be collected before the customer has labelled it and dropped it off, and so on. A series of events, each dependent on the previous one.

The TOC observes that in this chain of events, your throughput is only as fast as the slowest link in the chain. Imagine if you had a super-efficient pickup and sorting process that could collect and organise 500 parcels a day. That would be cool, but if your delivery infrastructure could only deliver 100 parcels a day, you'd have a bottleneck; those parcels would stack up high in your sorting centre. No matter how many parcels you pick up and organise, your throughput is only 100 parcels a day.

Similarly, if you pick up and drop off 100 parcels a day, but your sorting centre can only deal with ten, your throughput would be ten parcels a day. In this example, your parcels would be stacked up at the entrance to the sorting centre, with more and more pickups making the pile grow, while the delivery drivers would be staring at nearly empty vans, each containing only ten parcels a day to deliver.

Your customers would be unhappy that it is taking a long time to deliver their parcels (odds are that most customers' parcels would end up sitting in a pile for some time), and the money you'd be making in delivery sales would be mainly held up in inventory. In other words, you'll have taken the money, but not completed the majority of sales. It'll be costing you to hold all that inventory, and you'll also be paying delivery drivers to hang around waiting for parcels rather than delivering them.

The core premise of the TOC is that there are three elements we need to observe and manage:

1. Throughput (sales made and fulfilled)

2. Inventory (or work in progress (WIP))

3. Operating expense

Our primary aim in business according to these observations is to increase throughput, while simultaneously reducing inventory / WIP and operating expense as a secondary aim. The more sales we make and fulfil, the more profit we make, but we only make great profits if our operating expenses continue to reduce and we're not holding inventory – which is stuff we've paid to create but haven't shipped yet (and so haven't been paid for). In service businesses, we'll often refer to that as WIP.

We do this by recognising the bottlenecks in our process and elevating them, remembering that the throughput is only as fast as the slowest link. Focusing on the bottlenecks first is the way that we improve the performance of the entire chain of events. Once we've elevated each bottleneck and it's no longer a bottleneck, we repeat the process again and look for the new bottleneck, and so on.

Imagine a garden hosepipe. No matter how powerful the water pressure coming from the tap, the amount of water that can flow through the hosepipe is limited by its thickness. That's your inventory capacity – how many clients you can serve at one time. The higher your capacity, the more throughput (sales) you can manage.

Once you hit your inventory capacity, a bottleneck occurs. If we go back to the hosepipe analogy, the water will back up in the tap – you can't get any more through the hose. If there's a bottleneck in the hose (maybe it's twisted or something heavy is on top of it), then the capacity at that point is lowered. Past that bottleneck, the thickness of the hose is irrelevant; the amount of water that can flow through it is limited by how much can get past the bottleneck.

In your business, it's your job to check for all bottlenecks in your 'hose'; no work on increasing sales or fulfilment will make any difference to your delivery capacity once you've hit the constraints caused by those bottlenecks. Remove all the bottlenecks, and then it's a matter of checking the water pressure vs the thickness of the hose. If the water pressure isn't high enough to reach the capacity of the hose, then you need to raise that (work to increase sales). Conversely, if you're sending in more water than can pass through the hose at once, then you need to increase the thickness of the hose (expand your business's ability to process orders and deliver on its promises).

The three things work in tandem. Remove all bottlenecks, then either increase throughput (sales) or inventory capacity (the amount of work you can fulfil at once).

Business growth is the gradual increase of throughput and capacity, finding the slowest point in your processes – the bottleneck – and removing that constraint, and then looking for the next one, on repeat. Where you have a bottleneck, you must elevate that constraint to improve your operational efficiency. Improve operational efficiency, you improve momentum, selling more and making more with less effort.

How do you do that? The first step in the TOC is to *identify the constraint*. If we go back to our courier example, the sorting centre can process 500 parcels a day, but the delivery infrastructure can only deal with 100. It will have a pile of undelivered parcels, growing by 400 every day, and will never get through it. That's a whole load of parcels that aren't getting delivered. It's clear from the increasing stack of parcels in the delivery centre that the constraint – the bottleneck – is at that stage.

We could let systems thinking take over here. After a while, the courier firm is going to get a terrible reputation – 'They never deliver their parcels!' – and the number of customers will drop. When the daily number of parcels to be delivered drops to 100, the system will be in balance and the bottleneck will be gone, but the business will have lost a load of customers and there'll be people in the sorting centre kicking around, waiting for work.

Not ideal on any level. By bringing systems thinking into the analysis of that process, we can see there is a bottleneck we need to remove.

Move to step two: *exploit the constraint*. What Goldratt means by this is we should make sure that the processes running at the constraint are as efficient as possible; that there's nothing holding up the work in this area.

A deep dive into the delivery process is warranted here. How long is it taking drivers to make a round trip? Can we improve their navigation by ensuring they have a satnav or that the route delivers the parcels in the most efficient way? Are parcels split into groups in a single area so that the drivers aren't crossing each

other's boundaries? Do they need a co-driver to organise the route as they go and drop off the parcels while
the driver prepares for the next leg of the journey? Do
any of the drivers need additional training?

Using this courier example, you could likely think
of lots of ways that you could make the delivery process more efficient. Exploiting the constraint is a key
part of the TOC.

The next step can also be powerful: *subordinate
everything else to the constraint*. The TOC dictates that
you should move your resources to support the bottleneck. In the courier case, a simple solution would be
to move staff from the sorting centre into the delivery
department. This would reduce the number of parcels
sorted but have the potential to increase the number
of deliveries per day. That will reduce the pile in the
delivery centre and increase overall throughput.

Ensuring that the sorting centre organises parcels in
a way that is optimal for the delivery drivers is essential. You'll have optimised the delivery routes per van
in the previous step, so the sorting centre organising
parcels in piles appropriate to each van might take
more time but will speed up the delivery step.

The final step is to *elevate the constraint*. Once you've
moved staff from the sorting centre to the delivery
centre and ensured that the parcels are sorted in the
optimal way, then it's time to make sure that everything related to delivery is as effective as possible.

Some delivery vans may be waiting a long time
to be filled, perhaps because there are fewer parcels
for a particular region. In this case, it might be more

efficient to have smaller vans for those regions, so that the drivers don't have to wait so long until their vans are full. Alternatively, re-adjusting the routes to even out the load would improve performance. Ensuring that each driver is driving the shortest route between drop-offs by installing satellite navigation; providing customers with the ability to give precise directions to their houses and notes about where to drop off their parcels, alongside contact details so that the driver can call them before they get lost – these are ways that technology can improve performance at the bottleneck, so that the delivery process is as smooth as possible.

Technology can also free up resources. Automating the sorting process or applying a more intelligent region-tagging system at drop-off may allow more sorting centre staff to work in the delivery department instead.

This TOC process is a key step in your technology process, too. Once you've optimised as much as possible, you start again. What's the new bottleneck? When you've identified it, you can exploit the constraint, subordinate to it and elevate it. This entire process is an ongoing loop. Each time you complete a loop, you elevate the performance of your business.

A strategy for building effective software systems utilises systems thinking and the TOC together. It recognises the movement and flow of work, the reinforcing loops and the balancing loops, breaking that movement down into individual systems, and then identifying and elevating the bottlenecks within those systems.

Now that you have a sense of what we're going to be doing over the course of the rest of the book, we'll get started with the next step of the SCOPE framework, Clarify. This is where we're going to identify your bottlenecks by mapping out your team journey.

Here's where the fun begins. Let's get going!

5
Clarify

When you're deciding what sections of your systems to automate first, it can feel a little overwhelming to look at your entire business process workflow and try to imagine an automated version of it or an online application that handles the heavy lifting for you, especially if you have a business with twenty or more team members. By the time a business gets to that size, it has organically grown and enhanced its processes, and most likely has quite a few different systems running already.

This can often take the form of several connected third-party systems, along with a load of shared spreadsheets, usually held together by streams of processes in the heads of just one or two people. This kind of setup usually causes some amount of frustration – it worked fine when there were just five people in the business, but with more people comes more complexity, more lines of communication and more opportunities for agreed processes to be missed or inadvertently changed. It's also a dangerous setup.

When the systems or processes of an organisation are held in someone's head, should that person decide to move on or become unable to work for whatever reason, it can take months for the business to recover. Similarly, if you're reliant on a series of ever-expanding and increasingly complicated spreadsheets, or multiple systems held together by tenuous processes or manual tasks that must be learned and remembered, it only takes one person to leave or one spreadsheet formula to be broken or corrupted for unimaginable damage to be caused.

I spoke with a key leader in a global corporation recently and discovered that a vital process was run entirely on a huge, complex spreadsheet. This had started simply, and then grown beyond control. It's fragile and breaks easily, but no one dares amend it as the original creator of that spreadsheet has moved on from the company, and no one else knows exactly how it works.

The risk is real. We all need to either avoid getting to that point or gradually move away from it if we're already there.

That's why we will start this chapter with the journey map. The process creates a simplified view of the business and breaks it down into manageable components, based on the domain – the area of interest – and focusing in on the most important area to fix.

Journey mapping

The journey map shows the path that your customers take from discovering you, choosing to work with you or buy from you, through to your delivery of the product or service, post-sale support, follow-ups and so on. It's the roadmap of touchpoints made by you, your team and your customer.

Journey mapping is a fantastic way to understand how your business works. Of course, once you have a map of your journey, you can use it to identify common points of frustration for all parties, as well as opportunities to delight your customers, become more efficient and – yes – automate processes.

At Remote, we always start a software project off with journey mapping as part of our Clarity Workshops, even if we're clear on what we're going to build. Without fail, looking at the business journey in this way brings about insights and clarity, getting us focused on what needs to be developed first and what will give the client the biggest ROI in terms of increased revenue, increased savings and time saved within the business.

There are three ways to do this, depending on the energy and type of team you're working with. They are all similar, but the execution at the beginning is different.

Below, I've described the in-person version of journey mapping, but my team finds it's just as easy, if not better in some ways to do this online. When we do so, we connect via Zoom, and map out our journey using either miro.com or FigJam. From then on, the process is the same.

For in-person journey mapping, you'll need:

- A long roll of wallpaper (lining paper, that is, not the stuff that's printed on)

- Marker pens

- Assorted coloured Post-it notes – preferably yellow, red/pink, green and blue

- Adhesive tape that won't mark the walls of your office (if you care about that kind of thing)

Take the wallpaper and either unroll it over a large desk or table, or – my preference – tape it along a decent-sized wall in the office. If you can't get hold of lining paper, the Remote team has successfully run sessions with whiteboards and even a set of those funky glass partition walls in a co-working space.

Down the left edge of the paper, write a list of roles – what you write here will be different for everyone, and how you choose roles will depend on the size of your company. For example, for a medium to large company, you may write departments – Sales, Marketing, Accounts and so on – whereas for a small team, your roles might be names of team members – Dave, Linsey, Simon etc. However you assign your roles, be sure to put software and automation systems at the bottom, eg Xero, ActiveCampaign, our custom software etc.

With the roles written vertically down the left-hand side, draw horizontal lines across the paper, in between each name or department, creating 'swim lanes' for each role. Now clear the area of chairs and other desks so that your team has a decent-sized space to move around in.

You're ready. Attending the journey mapping session will be key stakeholders – ideally four or five. More than five in a session can get a bit too intense and progress may suffer, although it can also be productive and fun if the team members work together well, are entirely on the same page about how the journey mapping process works and are ready and willing to follow it closely.

By key stakeholders, I mean people who really know each aspect of the company domain. They're often in the roles I just described – one person who knows how all or at least most of the aspects of the sales process work; another from admin/operations; another from accounts, and so on.

To do this in a way that doesn't quickly descend into chaos (we've been there), appoint two roles for the session: facilitator and journey mapper. The facilitator will run and moderate the session, asking questions and making suggestions. The journey mapper will use the markers and Post-it notes to map the journey on to the wallpaper.

The facilitator starts with the very first touchpoint in your company – the first phone call, email or online lead generated by the customer – and works, step by step, through the entire path from order to fulfilment.

For each step, the facilitator asks 'What happens?', 'And then what happens?', and so on.

For each event that a member of the team suggests in response to these questions, the journey mapper writes it on a yellow Post-it note and places it on the paper in the correct swim lane, depending on who acts on the event. The Post-its will start on the left and move to the right as you progress chronologically through the journey. As the journey passes through specific milestones, say 'order received', 'order sent out' and so on, write the name of that milestone on a blue Post-it and place it at the top of the paper to mark that point in the journey, so that it's easy to follow the events when you look at it.

For example, you may have a blue Post-it note that reads 'order complete'. Below it in the Accounts swim lane, you may have a yellow Post-it reading, 'invoice sent to client', and another in the Operations swim lane reading, 'order marked as closed in the spreadsheet'.

I know, I know – we really don't want spreadsheets in our lives, especially to manage operations. That's likely why you're reading this book – you want to improve your automations and use easily manageable, sharable and intuitive software to mark your orders as closed – but the aim here is to map out your customer journey exactly as it is now, and not how you would like it to be ideally. That's a process for the next chapter!

It can take some time to map the journey as you need to cover every touchpoint. Everything that happens, from start to finish, needs to be in there. The beauty of the Post-its is that if you think of something later on in the session that should have been included, you can just shuffle them around to make space for the new event – so when you're placing them in the first place, be sure to leave a little space to allow for some re-jiggling later.

Now things can easily get rowdy. If you have confident people from admin who know the processes inside out, you can often get a stream of consciousness flowing from their brains into the room, and while that's gold, it can be quite an art to learn to slow them down and allow the journey mapper time to write all the Post-its. That's why the roles of facilitator and journey mapper are for two different people – when the energy rises, they'll need to work together to grab those nuggets of information as they flow.

Avoid getting into discussions about what works and what doesn't at this point. The aim is to methodically get all the events down on the Post-it notes. Trust the process and gradually walk through the journey.

As I mentioned, there are a couple of other versions of this section of Remote's workshop, depending on your thirst or otherwise for chaos and high-energy sessions. Firstly, rather than having a journey mapper, you can hand the yellow Post-it notes around the room and ask everyone to write events as they think of them and place them on the wallpaper. This works well when you have people who really enjoy interacting in the session.

For full high-energy mode, rather than starting at the beginning and moving through them in order, you can invite participants to just think of all the events that happen in the business and stick them randomly on the wallpaper. After everyone's out of ideas, you organise them into chronological order and see what's missing. This is less structured, and so can get out of control quickly, but sometimes that's just the kind of energy you need for an active, enjoyable and fulfilling journey mapping session.

Once you're done, you'll have a view of what happens in your business. Together, you and the stakeholders present should look through the journey map and see if there are any events that have been missed. You want to catch *everything* here.

When you all agree that you have everything noted, go through the map again, this time with your red and green Post-it notes at the ready. As your facilitator goes through the events one by one, the stakeholders are invited to suggest what the pain points are for each event. What I mean by that is the points of frustration that either members of the team or your customers feel when they encounter or take part in that event.

For the accounting team, for example, a pain point may be that a team member needs to copy order details from a sales spreadsheet into the accounts system. Another pain point may be that members of the sales team don't have an up-to-date view of stock levels, or what items a particular customer bought as part of their previous order. Note them all down on red Post-its and attach them to the relevant event.

Next, it's the turn of the gain points. These are opportunities for improvement or delight – write them down on your green Post-its. You'll often find that these feed off the pain points – if something is not working here, what would the opposite of that look like? What's the opportunity? Also be sure to note down things that work well as part of this process – you don't want to unnecessarily change things that are already optimal.

By this point in the process, you'll have a good idea of where you need to focus your efforts – the clusters of red notes will show you where the build-up of pain is and what needs to be improved most urgently. Remember the TOC – businesses tend to build up bottlenecks, and your operations will only be as fast and efficient as the slowest link in the chain of events.

It's my experience that the slowest link in the chain is often correlated with the biggest cluster of red Post-it notes. Over the next couple of chapters, we'll add a couple of layers to those notes so that you can get a sense of the priority each cluster should be given.

Now you have your journey map, you have a map of your potential for improvement. The next thing to do is to learn how to interpret what you're seeing, so you can work out how to make your processes better and what to automate.

Recognising the web of interdependencies

Understanding the intricacies of your journey map is pivotal. So far, we've discussed systems thinking and the TOC as lenses through which to view your business. Now let's turn our focus to a critical aspect of systems thinking: recognising interdependencies.

You've mapped out your process journey in a linear way. The steps are chronological, one happening after the other, but your business isn't linear. Imagine the journey like an intricate spider web. Each thread represents a touchpoint or sub-process – whether it's in marketing, sales or customer service. The spider at the centre of the web represents your customer.

As the spider moves along the threads, the whole web responds, with some threads bearing more weight than others. This web of interconnected touchpoints forms a complex, dynamic system. Any movement or change in one part of the web can affect the entire system, so understanding how these threads or sub-processes are interlinked is key to knowing where to focus your automation efforts.

Start by revisiting the detailed customer journey map you've created. While the map itself is a fantastic tool to outline the individual steps, it might not inherently show how these steps relate to each other.

Go beyond the surface; grab a marker and draw lines or arrows indicating relationships between each stage or component. For example, you might notice that a delay in the shipping process can put a strain on inventory storage. It may also lead to increased cancellation requests, putting pressure on both the customer service and finance departments to process refunds.

In another section, you may find that a cumbersome payment process doesn't just slow down the checkout, it increases the likelihood of abandoned carts. This in turn could lead to a surge in customer service enquiries as people struggle to complete their purchases.

These relationships between sub-processes can be of different types. Some are sequential, meaning one step must logically follow another. Others are parallel, occurring at the same time as one another. There might also be pooled interdependencies, where various departments or components work independently, but contribute to a larger shared goal. Understanding the type of relationship can help you assess the complexity of your business operations and identify constraints more effectively.

To prioritise the relationships that are the most impactful, assign weights or importance levels to each. For instance, take two sub-processes – the value of timely invoice payments versus maintaining a low error rate in orders. While both are crucial, prompt invoice payments might hold more weight because they directly affect your working capital and liquidity.

In the same way, weigh up the impact of minimising production downtime against that of an effective marketing campaign. While both will certainly contribute to profitability, minimising downtime might be more crucial as it reduces operational costs and maximises output, so you'd give that the higher weight.

Feedback loops play a pivotal role in systems thinking and interdependencies. A virtuous (positive) or vicious (negative) loop in one part of the business process can set off a chain of events that either improve or detract from the whole experience (more on these loops later in the chapter).

Let's say your clients are frustrated by slow contract approvals; this experience might make them think twice about extending their partnership with your organisation, affecting your long-term revenue streams. They might also share their grievances with other businesses in the industry, influencing your reputation and setting off a feedback loop that continually hurts your brand. Identifying these loops will help you understand where to make essential changes, allowing you to break a negative cycle or amplify a positive one.

Another point to watch for is competing objectives between different aspects of your business. For example, your finance team could be focused on cost-cutting measures to improve the bottom line, while your research and development department is pushing for increased investment in new technologies to fuel future growth. Both objectives are vital, but can pull the company in opposite directions, straining budgets and creating internal tension.

Identifying these conflicting goals early can help you map out a strategy that harmonises divergent priorities, paving the way for a balanced and effective operation. Those two attributes are essential for scale; you won't want to go too fast in a car if the back wheel is wobbling at slow speeds...

Leverage points

Once you've got a good understanding of your organisation's interdependencies, it's time to look for leverage points – the critical junctions in your customer journey where a small change could make a huge impact. These are the areas where an improvement to the process or an automated element could lead to substantial time and cost savings. It's my experience that elevating these leverage points usually leads to significantly improved customer satisfaction, too.

How do you identify and optimise your leverage points? Let's have a look.

Bottlenecks

Begin by examining your journey map for bottle-necks. We discussed bottlenecks in the previous chapter when we looked at the TOC. These are the areas where work gets backed up, delays accumulate and the entire process is slowed down. Bottlenecks are prime candidates for leverage points because resolving them can expedite multiple stages of the journey at once.

Say you notice that contract approvals often take longer than they should, causing a domino effect of delays. That's a clear leverage point. Addressing this could accelerate the entire operation, from customer onboarding to project delivery.

Decision-making moments

Another set of crucial leverage points revolves around decision-making moments – those critical times where a simple choice sets the course for what comes next. Take procurement as an example. The decision to purchase certain materials doesn't just influence your inventory, it also has a ripple effect on warehouse management, production schedules and even shipping logistics. Implementing software that automates the vetting and selection of vendors or materials can make this a powerful leverage point.

Software solutions at these moments of decision can streamline processes, reduce manual errors and ultimately free up valuable resources, setting off a cascade of efficiencies throughout your operation.

Interactions between sub-processes

As we've seen, your journey map isn't just a series of discrete steps; it's a complex web of interrelated activities. You need to recognise areas where different sub-processes intersect or rely on one another.

For example, how does the invoicing process relate to the cash flow? Perhaps speeding up invoicing could significantly improve cash flow, making it a strong leverage point. What about customer feedback? How does it influence product development? Finding a way to streamline feedback straight to the product team may be a strong leverage point, too.

In a business producing physical goods, the inventory management process is deeply interconnected with the sales process. Poor inventory tracking not only affects storage costs, but also has a direct impact on sales, making it another powerful leverage point.

Quantify the impacts

As you can see, leverage points create another web of cause and effect across your organisation. Identifying them is key to unlocking your organisation's ability to scale.

To validate the potential of each leverage point, you'll need to attach quantifiable metrics that can measure its impact. Is there a direct correlation between the identified leverage point and customer retention rates, for example? Does a certain leverage point dramatically reduce operational costs? Data-driven decision making is essential here. Gather as much information as you can about each leverage point you've identified, so that you can make smart decisions later.

Vicious and virtuous cycles

If you add momentum to a process that's in a reinforcing loop, you'll create more of whatever is in that loop. It's essential to get clear on the causes of bottlenecks and where the energy is flowing; identify reinforcing loops and mark out the ones that are causing issues;

follow the web of interdependencies back to find the root of the problem.

Spotting virtuous and vicious cycles means observing patterns and trends that lead to positive or negative outcomes reinforcing each other. A vicious cycle is essentially a self-perpetuating loop of actions and consequences that degrade the situation further with each iteration. Virtuous cycles lead to positive outcomes reinforcing each other, creating a loop of beneficial effects that build on each other over time. Unlike vicious cycles, which spiral situations downward, virtuous cycles promote sustainable growth and improvement. We harness and add momentum to virtuous cycles for scale.

Vicious cycles cause a business to fail. Virtuous cycles facilitate scale. Here are some strategies to identify these reinforcing loops.

Identify trends

Look for consistent patterns or trends that are leading to outcomes you don't want. Declining sales, decreasing productivity, increasing customer complaints and debtor days, rising employee churn – those are your vicious cycles.

Virtuous cycles are naturally the opposite. They could be anything from increased sales, improved customer satisfaction, higher employee morale, to enhanced productivity.

Analyse cause and effect

Once you've identified a trend, analyse the cause-and-effect relationships involved by scanning your web of interdependencies. Ask 'Why?' repeatedly to dig deeper into the root causes.

For example, if customer complaints are increasing, find out why customers aren't happy, then ask why those issues exist in the first place, and so on. Often, you'll find a chain of cause and effect that loops back on itself.

Look for feedback loops

Identify feedback loops that might be reinforcing a trend. A feedback loop happens when an outcome of a process influences the process itself and accelerates the trend.

If poor product quality leads to negative reviews, which in turn dissuade new customers from buying, resulting in reduced revenue for quality improvements, you've identified a reinforcing feedback loop that's contributing to a vicious cycle.

Observe system interactions

Understand how different parts of the system interact with each other. Sometimes, a vicious cycle might not be immediately obvious because it involves different departments or aspects of a business. For example, excessive cost-cutting measures might reduce prod-uct quality, affecting sales and leading to more cost-cutting in a detrimental loop.

Aligning with your larger business goals

It's important to take a step back while you go through the clarification processes described in this chapter. Make sure that the leverage points you've found align with your larger business objectives.

A change might be easy to implement and offer immediate benefits, but think about how it fits into the grand scheme of things. Will it help the business grow sustainably? Does it create more value than the effort spent on it? Does it free up your team to make more of an impact? The leverage points that are a yes to these kinds of questions should have a higher weighting and priority than the nice to haves. Nice to haves can be rabbit holes that entire departments fall down, at great cost and little benefit to the overall organisation. Avoid these rabbit holes.

We started the Strategise step in the SCOPE process by identifying your business's goals – its destination. You do that up-front so that you have a touchstone to refer to. Check back to those goals often, so that they're at the front of your thoughts as you identify feedback loops, leverage points, bottle-necks and opportunities.

Identifying leverage points in your journey map can be like finding the keys to a treasure chest of opportunities. Tweak these points, and you can set off a cascade of improvements throughout the business. By spotting bottlenecks, understanding decision-making moments, considering the complex web of interdependencies, quantifying the impacts and ensuring alignment with business goals, you can make targeted changes that yield substantial returns.

At the same time, understanding interdependencies is like having the blueprint of a building. It allows you to see the foundational structures that hold your business together and can guide your decisions on which areas to automate first. It ensures that your efforts are targeted, reducing the likelihood of unintended negative consequences.

As you keep these things in mind, weigh the interdependencies and leverage points, and mark the bottlenecks on your journey map with red Post-it notes. Where everything combines – a high weighting, a leverage point and measurable impact in alignment with the company's broader goals – you have the priorities for software to step in.

As we learned in the section on the TOC in the previous chapter, a business is only as strong as its weakest link, and our sales-to-fulfilment cycle is only as fast, effective and efficient as the slowest bottleneck in our system. Systems thinking shows us that our business is a system, which is a collection of many other systems.

The ongoing aim is to find the weakest of your current systems and improve that, and then do it again and again, gradually strengthening every aspect of the business and connecting each isolated system together. Eventually, you will have one overall system that is the centre of your business, the source of truth for your data and the key orchestrator of your operations, as well as the orchestrator of the dance between human and digital.

Your weakest link sits at the interconnection between five parts of your business workflow:

1. The one that has the highest number of red Post-it notes on your journey map

2. The one that slows down your operations across interdependencies – the bottleneck in your process

3. The one that is either the most frustrating or least satisfying to deliver for your team

4. The one that is repeated most frequently, consuming your time or that of your team

5. The one that has the most negative effect on the factors we talked about in the TOC section:

    - Increasing sales

    - Reducing inventory or WIP

    - Reducing overheads

When you scan your customer journey for these things, look for where there's an overlap of several of them. The more that overlap, the more likely it is that this is where you need to start.

The higher the weighting at these points, the more urgent it is to solve the problem. If you've done your information gathering, you should have metrics to hand now to see what actual effect the bottleneck is having on the company, in terms of both finances and other resources such as people or space.

6
Optimise Part 1 – The Optimal Journey

Welcome to the third step of the SCOPE framework, Optimise. As I'm sure you now realise, given that the tasks we covered in the previous chapter are ongoing, the opportunities to optimise the systems and processes in your business are almost infinite. To make the process manageable, this step is broken down into three parts, starting with identifying and enabling your optimal journey.

A business's growth is limited by its systems' capacity to support its operations. You've got clear on where you want your organisation to go and mapped out where you're at and what the most likely obstacles are to it running effectively. Your optimal journey will dramatically increase the capacity of your systems to support your operations and your ability to scale.

You now need to create a new map of the ideal journey from start to finish for the process you've identified as a priority. If you're aiming for the biggest bottleneck/opportunity first, this will be the section of your map that has the highest number of red Post-it notes, the highest weightings of impact and the most related interdependencies.

The aim is to create a new process that can stand alone and relies on the other processes as little as possible; this in software is called 'separation of concerns'. The more you can abstract out your systems into individual processes, the less tangled they are with the other systems and the easier they are to maintain and improve.

This new process must be as simple as possible (but no simpler). You ensure this by analysing each step in the process and asking, as entrepreneur, author and lifestyle guru Tim Ferriss says (2023), 'What would this look like if it were easy?'

The answer to this question may be different for each step. For ageing systems or processes that have organically developed over time, you may find that you have steps in there that aren't needed any more, or that were put in to satisfy a particular bureaucratic demand that no longer exists. Simplify by removing as many non-essential steps as possible – duplication or copying and pasting of data, unnecessary signoffs and so on. You don't want anyone having to download or copy and paste data into a separate document or system if you can possibly help it.

An important element to watch out for is the human bottleneck. If a process relies on someone manually completing a task, then a bottleneck will form when they have more work than they can handle. The nature of business means that the person won't just have that one job to do, either – they'll be fitting it in with other demands. If it's possible that a software solution could replace the manual one, you've just released a bottleneck.

When you find a human bottleneck, consider how this bottleneck might be replaced with a software equivalent that's better than the human version. In this chapter, we'll look at the main ways to do so, with examples of how they might solve particular bottlenecks.

Portals

Customer portals:

- Allow customers to place orders directly instead of by email or on the phone

- Allow customers to specify work requests and create automatic quotations

- Provide document downloads to reduce requests for documentation

- Show the status of orders, along with any details such as deadlines and progress

- Provide onboarding or information about how to work with you

- Show financial information such as invoices and related costs for your product/service

This solves problems like:

- Orders being sent in by email, and then copied into a management system by customer service staff

- Documents being printed out for archiving or to be signed by a particular stakeholder

- Printing out booking or order forms to send to clients to fill in

- Needing to personally make sales calls to take an order when the customer is already converted and just needs to place the order

- Manually drafting customised versions of the same report or proposal repeatedly for different customers

- Manually onboarding new clients with in-person walkthroughs

Team portals

A central hub for all the information required to run the operations of the company, a team portal dramatically improves communication between people and increases the efficiency and effectiveness of every task. This will have similar features to the customer portal, but from a team perspective. It:

- Shows inbound customer orders

- Displays financial information for products, services and customers

- Shows the status of orders, along with any team member who has been assigned to tasks, and allows that status to be updated and reassigned to different team members

- Displays any ongoing communication with clients around orders

- Holds the latest version of all required documents

This solves problems like:

- Sales teams with no oversight on inventory numbers being forced to guess orders, and then go back and amend them once the actual numbers have been confirmed

- Team leaders being forced to manually check order status regularly to make sure that customers are kept up to date with progress

- Manually looking up or calculating numbers for quotations or reports

- Team members needing to personally check with other team members whether they've completed tasks due to lack of oversight

- Team members needing to collate documents/resources/assets from different undocumented locations to manually send to customers

- Sales staff manually taking orders by phone or email rather than providing software systems to take those orders

- No way to keep track of leads or orders once they're created

---

CASE STUDY

An accountancy client approached us to tackle a bottleneck in their payroll department. Previously, their clients submitted payroll information via spreadsheets – sometimes monthly, sometimes weekly. This data had to be manually entered into the client's Sage system, a process fraught with errors and inefficiencies. Two bookkeepers were tied up per payroll, with one typing and the other checking for mistakes.

Our solution was to build a portal allowing clients to enter payroll information directly into the system. This application validated the data and posted it straight into Sage Payroll, drastically cutting down the time required of each bookkeeper.

The portal offered a faster, more intuitive experience for clients, eliminated the processing bottleneck and freed up bookkeepers to work in other critical areas.

The payroll department transformed from that making the biggest loss in the business to the most profitable division. With the new system, our client could take on many new payroll customers without incurring additional overheads.

Workflow or process automation

In this context, automation is the 'If this, then that' aspect of your software. Let's run through a few general examples to give you an idea of what I'm talking about:

- If a customer posts a support request, then automation sends a direct notification to the support team.

- If a customer reaches the end of their trial period, then automation creates a new task for the sales team to follow up with a call.

- If I change the status of a lead to won and assign the contact a client tag, then automation puts them on the client newsletter list.

- If a contact is assigned a client tag, then automation sends them the client welcome pack.

- If someone pays an invoice, then automation marks the relevant ticket in the project as paid.

- If it's the end of the month, then automation compiles a report of all tasks completed this month for each client and sends these reports to the project manager.

- If a document is approved, then automation sends an email to the delivery team to let them know that they're ready for the next step in the process.

- If a particular piece of information is entered in a form, then automation sends the data via an API to a third-party package.

- If I upload a spreadsheet of data, then automation does some calculations and produces a report.

These tasks are simple and repeatable, and automation of them saves a huge amount of time when it's stacked up and used across the entire company. There are so many small tasks we do every day that we could delegate to software, but they're often so embedded into 'how I do this' that we don't think about whether a computer could pick up the slack. Examples include keeping team members or customers up to date with progress, keeping ourselves in the loop with logistics, providing prompts on work that needs to be done in the right order at the right time, and taking data from one place and putting it somewhere else to avoid copying and pasting or looking up.

Third-party software like Zapier or Make.com can connect multiple systems together, providing automation between machines in the background. Good custom or single-system platforms will include automation too, sending out emails to our customers or keeping records updated while we get on with the stuff we're good at, and our team members get on with the work that actually requires human connection and creativity.

Spotting the tasks that can be completely automated like this is a key part of your analysis of the operations journey. It might take some investment in terms of time and/or money to set it up, but once it's done, you and your team don't have to worry about it again, and that task can be performed ten or even 100 times more frequently than when you did it manually, with no extra time or cost spent by you or your team.

When you go through each step in your journey, your first question should be 'Could software do this task for me?' This is the leap in mindset that prevents us from struggling to scale or keep up with demand. It's what holds us together as our businesses grow and prevents them from losing margins when we need to ramp things up. When done right, our automated processes are the never-tired, never-bored, never-complaining army of workers that keep our businesses running smoothly, can handle any number of clients and earn money while we sleep.

Reporting and data analysis

Analysing and reporting on the data you have in your organisation is often the very reason you'll need to use software in the first place, and so it is by its nature spread throughout most applications. In this context, however, I'm talking about collating and presenting the information you have in a way that allows for you to make informed decisions on progress and strategy.

Collecting large amounts of data on stock, projects, tasks or sales, for example, is useful, but you'll soon find that you have too much to simply browse through. You need to be able to pull sections of it out, filter it at several intersections, perform calculations on it or refine it to find the one piece of information you need, or to understand and interpret what the data is telling you about your business. By defining the 'shape' of the data, your software systems can understand how it needs to be displayed for you and what calculations can be done with it, and you can save hours, days, even months of your teams' valuable time as a result.

CASE STUDY

'How much stock do we have across all our brands and where is that stock physically, right now?' is a question one of Remote's global clients asks every year. Of course, they need a reliable answer, but after decades of acquisitions, consuming brands with their own systems and methods for managing and tracking stock that didn't talk to each other, and with factories and ports and showrooms all over the UK, that answer took a single employee an entire year to complete. They needed to compile the data across many spreadsheets, and then manually compare and interpret that data, creating a large stock report.

When that person retired, our client commissioned
Remote to create a system that would perform the job
automatically, and much more effectively. The solution
we delivered included a portal for collecting the data, an
email and automated username-and-password system
for chasing up the data from admins and employees,
and a comprehensive reporting system that would
analyse the results and find data anomalies with enough
information for the admin team to investigate and solve
them. The system reduced the data collection time from
several weeks down to one weekend; the data analysis
and reporting time down from several months to
minutes; and the manual investigation time down from
a year to two months.

That's the power of data collection and analysis.
When written well, software systems can find and
analyse data in a way that's simply not possible with
the human mind. We can't take in millions of rows
of numbers and find variations and mistakes anywhere near as efficiently or effectively as a piece of
dedicated software.

It's not just about big data, though. Reports that are
automatically collected and delivered can give you at-
a-glance performance stats, from sales data to metrics.
How many leads came in this week? How many did
you convert? Are you up on this year, or down? Why?
How's your financial performance? What's your next
tax bill going to be? All of these questions are easily
answered at a glance when you have the right software
in front of you. When you have your collected data in
place using the methods we've discussed previously,

this kind of analysis and reporting is easy to do, can save you hours and keeps your business on track.

Reports will come in several flavours. There's the more traditional type that you most likely think of when I say 'report' – a page of numbers, summaries and analysis – but there are also different views of the data, which might form dashboards of key metrics and tasks to do and completed. We at Remote always aim to give our clients 'sleep at night' dashboards, which provide a single page that contains the numbers they need to know as business leaders so they can rest easily in their beds without any unanswered questions or concerns. In fact, we found this kind of dashboard so useful that we created Vaulta.io, a dedicated platform to build them for companies.

These different views of your data help you to understand and manipulate it easily. A great example is the Kanban board, invented by Toyota engineer Taiichi Ōhno (Kanban Tool, no date). A set of vertical columns representing different stages of your sales pipeline or product/service delivery, it uses cards – sticky notes, postcards, or digital rectangles – to represent tasks or leads, or jobs that start in the far-left column and are moved to the right as they progress.

This gives you an instant view of where you're at with that pipeline. Where are jobs piling up? How many leads do you have waiting for proposals? How many tasks have the team completed this week?

The Kanban board is a great software migration from the original TOC idea. The board is your assembly line, and each step is now a column on the board.

In studying the TOC, we look at the different stops on the assembly line to see where items are piling up – the bottleneck. With a Kanban board, we can see which column has the longest stack of cards assigned to it.

Gantt charts are another example (Gantt.com, no date). Usually the realm of project managers, this chart is a timeline of all the planned tasks of a project – each one is listed in a row, and the length of time it should take is indicated by a horizontal bar. The longer the task will take to perform, the longer the bar. Lining up these bars in chronological order across the chart shows how much time the project will take in total. The chart can be used as an organic always-up-to-date indicator of project progress; you can see whether you're behind or ahead, and what tasks depend on others.

It's this kind of at-a-glance data analysis that can give us the edge with our business. As more of our work becomes digital, we can't see where our company is by simply looking at our team members sitting behind their computers and judging how well we're doing. We need the data displayed in front of us in a way that we can see what's actually happening in the background. This empowers us as leaders to make the right decisions at the right time and keep our business thriving.

Integrations

Software systems rarely work in isolation. They usually work in collaboration with other systems, too. Your software needs to play nicely with others, so that data flows smoothly and invisibly without human intervention. Sending data back and forth between all your systems automatically is the key to stopping duplications and the typo problems caused by people copying data from one place to another by hand.

Moving data around using software is faster, cheaper and more accurate than people doing so. You start by identifying some of the most common systems that your business may want to integrate with, such as accounting software, CRM software and inventory management systems.

Let me give you some context. The first system most businesses adopt, after perhaps email and word processing, is an accounting package – Xero, Sage and QuickBooks are the most popular. Over a period of years, these packages will have built up multiple features and collected vast amounts of your data. You don't want or need to pay a development company to build you a custom accounting software package unless you've got an extremely good reason to do so, but you might want your new system to use those packages on your behalf, creating and sending invoices, for example, or recording sales.

A good number of businesses still have teams copying their invoices by hand from email into their accounts package and adding sales lines manually. When you're running your business with the help of a custom system, that can all happen behind the scenes, freeing your exhausted administrator to do something more useful with their time.

It's the same with CRM systems. Your mailing lists and sales pipelines can easily benefit from integration with your core system, and vice versa – keeping your mailing lists up to date when new customers sign up, or keeping notes on sales and issues up to date where customer service teams and sales staff can easily see them.

Methods of integration

There are three methods that software developers use to hook you up: APIs, webhooks or third-party integration platforms. I'm going to run through them now so that you can understand what your developer is talking about when you're telling them you need to connect to Xero, for example.

APIs are the most common type of interface. An API works like a bridge between two systems, allowing them to send and receive data in a standardised way.

Think of a waiter in a restaurant. The waiter takes your order and delivers it to the kitchen; similarly, an API takes requests for information from one program and sends it to another. Just as the kitchen staff prepares the food and gives it back to the waiter to serve to you, the second program uses the API to send back the requested information to the first program.

What's cool about APIs is that only essential information is shared between systems. In the restaurant analogy, the customer doesn't need to know how to cook the food – the kitchen staff could even be communicating to each other in a different language – and the kitchen team doesn't need to know anything about how to collect orders from the customers at the table. The waiter, like an API, is the interface between them.

This process is standardised and streamlined, which means that it's efficient and reliable. As long as the order is written on the waiter's notepad in a way that both parties can understand, the system will work seamlessly. APIs work just the same, even if they were created by different developers or companies, using different languages or infrastructure.

Webhooks are similar to APIs, with one crucial difference. APIs facilitate two-way communication. The waiter gives the order to the kitchen staff and the kitchen staff gives the waiter the food to serve to the customers in return, but in real life, it doesn't generally happen like that unless it's in a hyper-efficient fast-food restaurant.

Usually, the waiter gives in the order, and then there's a delay while the kitchen staff cook the food. The waiter will then need to go back to the kitchen every few minutes to ask if the food is ready. Of course, in real life, the chef shouts 'Service!' or pings a bell, and the waiter knows that the food is ready, collects it up and serves it to the customer.

That's a webhook. It sits and waits for a trigger – the bell in our example. Once the trigger is fired, the webhook springs into action. In the analogy, the waiter collects and serves the food, but in a real software system, a webhook might send an email to notify your client that their order has been shipped or update your database so that the information is current.

Webhooks can sit and wait for days or weeks at a time – they don't mind, it's what they do. They wait for a notification, and then act. It's a one-way thing, though, and that's the main difference between webhooks and APIs.

In the example, the webhook would be used to send a one-way notification from the kitchen to the customer (or waiter), whereas the API (the waiter) would be used to facilitate two-way communication between the customer and the kitchen. Both the webhook and API can be used in different ways to facilitate communication between different systems, depending on the specific needs of the situation.

The third-party integration platform is, under the bonnet, the same as the first two, but it's a more user-friendly way of managing them. APIs and webhooks are bread and butter for a software developer, but can't be used by anyone else. They're too complicated unless you're a developer yourself.

Platforms like Zapier, Make or Microsoft Flow aim to make communication more accessible. They provide a drag and drop interface that allows you to do your own data mapping, and in turn, they manage the API and webhook handling for you. They're a neat way of connecting something up quickly, and if you're tech-savvy but not a developer, they can save you some expenses.

At Remote, we set these platforms up for our clients occasionally, but we much prefer to code APIs and webhooks directly, for one reason...

Integration challenges

Let's go back to our waiter as API analogy. Imagine the chef updates the menu. The waiter must be informed about the change; if they're not, they could carry on taking orders from the old menu and the kitchen might not be able to fulfil these orders. Also, the customers wouldn't be made aware of the new dishes available, so would miss out on some opportunities.

Similarly, data structures can change and the APIs need to be kept up to date. A solid API versioning system needs to be put in place, tracking and managing changes so that you don't have the equivalent of two waiters with different menus taking orders in the same restaurant.

Keeping these systems up to date is an important part of maintenance and a reason why third-party integration systems like Zapier can be challenging to use in a production environment; they'll often simply stop working if one of the parties changes their API without a solid versioning system in place (I'm looking at you, PayPal). Integration via APIs isn't always possible; it relies on the third-party platform having support from its developers to keep the API in place and up to date. Some systems simply don't build this in. If you do integrate your system with a third party, make sure you have ample monitoring in place to inform you if it changes or goes down, and that your system will fall back gracefully when that happens.

A final word about security. This is, of course, of paramount importance throughout the whole of the development process, but it's of particular importance when you're integrating with third parties.

Imagine if our waiter was naïve and took an order from one customer, and then believed that customer when they said a different table would be picking up the bill. It would be equally awkward if some smart Alec found a way to send fake orders into the kitchen, and the chefs started delivering all sorts of food to nobody at all.

That's similar to what can happen if your APIs aren't secure. API keys are the digital equivalent of the key to your front door; an API key identifies the person talking to the waiter and proves that they are who they say they are. Keeping those keys safe is as important as keeping a real key safe. Your APIs require secure keys as much as your shiny new front door, which you wouldn't leave unlocked and open for anyone to walk in.

Artificial intelligence and machine learning

It's only in the last couple of years, at the time of writing, that the wonders of AI have been available for utilisation in our platforms in an accessible form. Before that, if the Remote team wanted to develop a machine learning (ML) platform, we'd have to code it ourselves, and then train it with tens or hundreds of thousands of data points.

All that has changed. Text/image generation, transcription, analysis and summarisation/categorisation features are now easier to build into your software system than many of us ever believed would be possible. AI opens up whole new worlds to us all, so let's talk about what that means for your business.

Before we do, let's get clear on what I mean by AI. It contains a subset of technologies, of which ML is just one. Others include natural language generation and natural language processing, robotics, autonomous agents and vehicles. Each of these subsets has its own unique applications and possibilities.

For our purposes, we'll focus on ML, specifically on a branch of it called deep learning, which is what powers the technology known as generative pretrained transformers (GPT). This is the area of AI that's developing at a rapid pace and being integrated into all types of software with incredible results.

Large language models (LLMs) use ML to produce and read human-like text. They learn patterns in data and can generate text that is remarkably similar to human-written prose. As I write this, the most advanced version is GPT-4o, developed by OpenAI. GPT models were originally developed to perform language translation but have expanded to achieve things that felt like science fiction just a few years ago.

You've almost certainly already interacted with an LLM, perhaps without realising it, whether it's a customer service chatbot or predictive text on your phone. LLMs power many of these interactions. You may have used the implementation of LLMs that's got a lot of people excited – ChatGPT.

What's important about ChatGPT and similar LLMs such as Anthropic's Claude or Google's Gemini? I believe that AI is going to permeate every part of our lives over the next few years, but its power is available right now. At Remote, we're integrating it into all of the projects we're building at the moment – it has so many benefits and the results can be astonishing.

How can you leverage this powerful technology into your business? Here are some examples.

Customer service

Provide immediate responses to customer enquiries 24/7 via chatbots, reducing the workload on your customer service team and increasing customer satisfaction. AI can handle simple queries and forward more complex issues to a human agent. This technology can also help with guiding customers through troubleshooting steps, providing product recommendations and much more.

Internal processes

AI can be used to automate many repetitive tasks within your organisation. For instance, it can schedule meetings, organise emails, manage tasks and more. It can also analyse large sets of data and provide insights that would be difficult to discern otherwise. An AI agent can take a complicated instruction, work out the steps to complete the task, and go about following its own steps by web browsing, filling in forms and even writing and debugging code.

Product/service delivery

AI can be used to improve the delivery of products or services. It can predict demand, optimise supply chain logistics and help manage inventory more effectively. It can also personalise products or services based on customer preferences and feedback.

Content generation

LLM technology can be used to generate content for your business. This could be in the form of articles, social media posts or product descriptions. It can even help in brainstorming ideas, creating plans and writing personalised email marketing campaigns.

Business analysis

AI can quickly analyse vast amounts of business data to provide actionable insights. It can predict trends and perform market analysis and help in decision making.

AI is no longer a tool only for large corporations; it has practical applications for businesses of all sizes.

As technology continues to improve and become more accessible, it will be an essential part of any business looking to scale effectively.

It's important to remember that AI is a *tool* and not a solution in and of itself. Think of it as a sidekick – the Robin to your Batman. You define what it does and how it does it, and it carries out those instructions for you while you move on to the next opportunity.

It's there to enhance human capabilities, not replace them. I like to say that with AI – and actually, all of the software implementations we're talking about in this book – we can take ten people and help them have the impact of 100, rather than reducing the team down to one and have that person do the work of ten.

Successful AI implementation isn't just plug and play. It requires a deep understanding of your business processes and a clear strategy. It's not about using AI for AI's sake; it's about having the best tools to solve the challenges you're facing as you scale and implementing the right software for the right task.

In the coming years, businesses that embrace AI and adapt it into their operations are likely to gain a significant competitive edge, whether it's through improved efficiency, increased customer satisfaction or access to deeper insights. AI holds enormous potential to transform businesses. If you're not utilising that potential now, I strongly suggest you actively look at how you might do so.

That said, while the benefits of AI are immense, it's essential to consider the ethical implications of its use, such as data privacy and bias in its decision making. Understanding these factors and implementing responsible AI practices will be crucial for the successful integration of it into your operations.

AI, and specifically LLMs, offers exciting opportunities. It can streamline processes, improve customer service and provide valuable insights. Its effect on every industry is going to be huge in the coming years, but there's concern among many that AI could take their jobs.

I'd suggest that AI won't take your job, but someone who's successfully utilising AI may do. Stay sharp and look for opportunities when you're working through the SCOPE framework that we're walking through together here.

7
Optimise Part 2 – Optimised Workflows

B y now, you should have a good sense of the kind of solutions your software will provide. You will most likely need a combination of the software types we discussed in the previous chapter collecting data and documents, analysing them, reporting on them and allowing you to change them easily to track the progress of your product or service delivery.

To identify the specific tasks you need your software to perform, look at the overall process and ask what its ultimate outcome should be. Then take each step in the journey of that process and ask four questions:

1. Why do we do this?

2. Do we have to do this?

3. Could this be simpler?

4. Does this directly contribute to the ultimate outcome of the process?

As you do this with each step, note down the simplest, least-time-intensive, preferably-done-with-software method to getting the outcome you want. By relating each step to the ultimate outcome, you're adopting a purpose-first approach – noting the primary purpose of the outcome and making sure that you only carry out tasks that directly move towards that purpose. If the task at hand doesn't directly move towards the purpose, then you need to question its existence altogether.

If a task does indeed move you towards the ultimate outcome, then ask if it needs to be done by a person or if it could be done by software. An alternative question to this may be, could it be simplified or altered in a way that would mean software could do it?

For example, are you taking information from phone calls or emails and copying it into a spreadsheet or order system? Do you really have to print out that order form? Could you create an online order form that customers could fill in instead? Do you have to copy that information into the accounting package? Could the system that holds that information send the information to the package directly and automatically? Could you use or build a system that does that?

If you had a dashboard that showed the status of each order for every customer, would it mean that management could make more informed decisions, the customers wouldn't need to call in to ask about their orders and every member of the team could work more efficiently, knowing what is coming in and when? Could a software system automatically generate a report or proposal or document and send it to the customer on a scheduled or on-demand basis?

Could you create a repository of all your assets, so that every member of the team knows exactly where to go to find the right documents? Could you create a workflow that prompts team members to perform tasks at the precise moment they need to be done, rather than waiting for someone to remember to do those tasks? Could you automate the tasks altogether?

Some of these optimisations will be obvious and others will depend on you having a general knowledge of what's possible. Later, I'll give you the information you need to understand the difference.

Re-humanising

When we're automating, our task isn't to dehumanise the process. We don't want to remove people from our processes altogether; the aim is to make sure that software is doing the tasks that people don't have to do, so that they are free to do the work that needs the human touch.

Ultimately, when we're freed up from the meaningless admin or simple stuff, we're *re*-humanising the process. It gives us a chance to really connect with our suppliers, our team and our customers. Think of the number of occasions you could have made a personal phone call to a key client, but perhaps didn't have the headspace or the time because of all the urgent rather than important tasks you had to do.

When you're examining your processes for opportunities to automate, what you'll quickly discover is that your bottlenecks or constraints will tend to fall into one of these categories. Team members will be:

- Manually copying data from one place to another

- Printing things out, or receiving printed documents and having to copy information back into a system

- Repeating the same tasks, which could be automated, over and over

- Manually performing admin tasks that could be performed by software

- Creating documents that could be generated with minimal (or no) human input

- Completing steps in the process that are no longer necessary

- Collecting information from disparate places (because there's no single source of truth for your data) when it could be collected and calculated for you by software

- Manually tracking and managing the status of projects or deliverables with no central resource or dashboard

- Having to relay the same information to someone repeatedly (eg customer or employee onboarding, training or standard operating procedure information)

- Being the 'middleware' between two parties when software could orchestrate the process on your behalf (taking order calls from customers who could easily be using a portal or order system is a common example of this)

- Performing a task for a customer or supplier that doesn't require human elements such as relationship building, empathy, compassion, creativity or intuition

These candidates for automation give you a map towards your ideal workflow and system. The task now is to create a new journey map, listing out the steps in your amended process, but with the automation candidates replaced with your new alternatives, managed by software. For example:

- Where you previously copied data from one place to another, it is now entered or copied into the correct place by software. (APIs were built for this.)

- Where a document was put in place by hand, it's now generated by a software-driven document creation process, based on a template and your input.

- Where you had to send information to others, the information is now collated and sent automatically.

- Where one party entered some information, and you then passed it on to another party or mediated between the two, an application now acts as the interface between them. (Think Airbnb taking the place of holiday rental agents.)

It's important not to be concerned right now with how this software is going to be built – you need to stay in strategy mode, focusing on the outcomes you want. You're not interested in going to the level of 'a button goes here, and when I click that, this happens over here' and so on; you're interested much more with 'when we send this parcel out for delivery, the customer receives an email with the tracking number so that they can follow its progress' or 'when a customer signs up, they receive a series of welcome emails, one every day, walking them through how we work'.

This focus on outcomes is essential. You want to find the shortest line between two points and you do that by keeping the end – the outcome – in mind. If you're not sure on what that end is, look at the existing process and perform the five whys exercise, developed in the 1930s by Japanese inventor Sakichi Toyoda. The principle is to ask why five times, each why referring to the previous answer.

Asking why repeatedly in this way brings you back to the flip side of purpose-first principles. When you truly understand why you're doing a particular thing, you can aim directly for that outcome. This strips away bureaucracy and helps you streamline your workflow, removing needless steps and making sure that you only get involved personally when that human touch is necessary to add genuine value to the team or customer experience; when a step in the process requires elements of human interaction and isn't just a formality or something that you do because you've always done it.

Another reason why you don't get into the technical 'how' details at this point is because when you come to work with a software team or a no/low code solution like Autm.io, the process is way easier. You're also open to new possibilities for optimisation if you focus on your end result and don't have a fixed idea that you need a button here, a popup there or a page that does this or that.

When you're clear on the outcome and able to articulate it without any strong opinion on how it will be achieved, the creative possibilities are wide open for anyone in the team – or your existing software system – to solve. That's a perfect recipe for true innovation.

Your new business journey

Go through each step in your original business journey and draw a new journey below it. Either keep each step because it works, replace it with a digital process or remove it altogether.

You may find that in some cases, several manual steps in the journey can be replaced by a single step or process thanks to software managing the task. In other instances, you may still have the same number of steps, but the touchpoints are improved. For example:

- The customer sends you an order by email

- The sales rep copies the details of the order into your order form

- The sales rep emails the order form to customer service

- Customer service copies the order into the orders system

Might be replaced with:

- The customer enters the order into your orders system using a customer portal or sends a purchase order by email which is intercepted and interpreted by AI

- The order is saved into the orders system

- The sales rep either approves the order or phones the customer to confirm the order and up-sell where possible

- Sales and fulfilment are automatically sent an email, notifying them of the order

Both versions are four-step processes, but in the second version, none of those steps are carried out by a member of the team, apart from the option of the salesperson making a call to improve the relationship with the customer or increase the order. That is now a purely human task, with the sales rep using the time automation has freed up for them for a one-to-one phone call with the customer. This is a clear example of how automating a process brings the human element back into the business operating system.

Go through each step, checking for the bottlenecks we've discussed, and rewrite it using the best optimised workaround for each one. This ensures that where a digital version of the step is possible and appropriate, it's used. Remember, you're not concerned with the how, only the intended outcomes.

Let's look at some examples. Where data is copied and pasted by hand, ensure that it is either typed directly into the correct system or an automated process sends the data to that system. Question the need for multiple systems – they're usually a sign of a static fixed solution that requires workarounds rather than an evolving solution that works in line with the company's preferred way of doing things.

When documents are being printed out, question the need for this. If possible, replace these documents with those held online as PDFs or web pages and signed with a digital signing service. Where documents are created by hand, use software to generate them, either as a process within a custom system or using a dedicated third-party tool for your industry.

If a task is repeated and it doesn't involve human touch elements like building relationships, using innovation or intuition, and so on, question whether software could perform that task instead. Where tasks are no longer necessary, remove them.

Where data needs to be collected from disparate sources, utilise APIs to store it in one place for easy retrieval and reporting. When data needs to be analysed, interpreted, collated or reorganised in some way, implement AI to do this as part of the data flow. If information about how a process is performed is relayed either repeatedly or in a way that's reliant on memory or information from different sources, store the information for the appropriate steps either in a wiki (a site that can be edited by multiple users) or, even better, as a series of video instructions.

Where it's difficult to track the status of projects or orders, use a dashboard to display all the important information in one place and allow your customers to log into a customer-facing version so that they can check whenever they feel the need. If you or your team members are acting as mediators between two parties, orchestrate notifications and facilitation using software dashboards and forms that both parties can log into and use.

Follow each of your original bottlenecks in turn with a focus on the required outcome. When you've created a new flow for all the outcomes, you'll have a map of your ideal journey. You may want to go through it a couple of times to make sure that you have a sense of how the process will flow and whether there may be new bottlenecks revealed that you could replace.

Remember, this is just one flow in the overall process – one thing that needs to be done. You're not trying to cover everything that you and your team do in your business, just a particular step or system that is causing frustration. Once you've been through the whole process for the biggest bottleneck, you'll be able to loop back around and perform the task again with the next-most-important bottleneck, and so on until your entire business operating system is running smoothly and making the most of all the benefits that software has to offer.

In the next chapter, I'll show you how to turn this new journey map, this flow, into a format that can be easily followed by developers. Equally as important, we'll cover how to break up each step in the map and discriminate between aspects of functionality necessary for your software and ideas which aren't a priority.

It may be challenging to come up with your digital alternatives right away as you first need to understand what's possible. The next chapter will walk you through that too, so don't worry, I've got your back, but if you find yourself getting stuck with this stage or are unsure how to solve the issues that you come across, contact me via my website. You will also find several examples of ideal journey maps on the resources page https://paulmcgillivray.com/resources so you can see what one looks like. Be sure to take the scorecard (linked from that page) too; it'll show you what areas you may need to focus on first and give you some guidance on where to start.

How to build the right thing, first time

What we've just done is jump into the entrepreneur mindset. It may already be familiar to you or it may be the first time that you've thought about your business in this way. Either way, it delivers a challenge, one that it's important to get our heads round and resolve.

You see the vision for your business. You may already see what a software application would need to do to help you achieve that vision (if you're not there yet, don't worry; the next chapter will show you what's possible). You know what you're aiming for and have a sense of what you need to create to get there.

If you've really given yourself permission to dream, your vision is *huge*. The difference you could make in the world is epic and life changing, and the software you'd need to build to deliver the reach and capacity to get there could be equally substantial.

This is a problem. The chances are that you'd need to invest a large sum of money to get this software built. It'll take time as well as the financial investment, and you don't know if your customers will use the software, if the team will adopt it or, perhaps most importantly, whether your assumptions about what it will take to get you where you need to go are even correct.

Here's the bottom line. It's all an assumption. Guesswork. However informed you are, however much experience you have in your industry or business domain, your idea remains an assumption until you put it in the hands of whoever's going to use it and get their feedback.

As a result, it's seriously unwise to build the whole thing at once; to spend tens or hundreds of thousands of pounds and months of work before testing that your assumptions are correct. Because if they're not – particularly if the first assumption at the base of all the others is wrong – then all your time, work and money will have been wasted.

Let's make sure that doesn't happen. The key is often a challenge for an entrepreneur who sees and is excited by the big vision and wants to get there immediately:

We start small.

As small as possible, but no smaller.

The next chapter will show you how.

8
Optimise Part 3 – Keeping It Lean

You've got your ideal business journey all mapped out. It's an exciting time when it's all too easy to get carried away and try to run before you can walk. In this chapter, we'll look at how to ensure your enthusiasm is well placed and your vision is realised to optimal effect.

The minimum viable product (MVP) is your safeguard against loss and the bringer of confidence to your business. It answers the singular question: 'Is this assumption correct?'

To find your MVP, define what assumption you need to prove and build the smallest amount of software you require to prove it. For example, let's say your base assumption is 'My business operations will be greatly accelerated by an online portal that takes customers' orders and processes them using software, giving the right members of my team the right information right away, and keeping my customers updated on their deliveries' progress'. It's a sound and common assumption, but at its root is the assumption that your customers will be happy to enter their orders into an online portal, rather than sending you an email or phoning them in.

In this case, the MVP would start here – testing that assumption. If you don't, you might build an entire customer portal that none of your customers will use, and then you've wasted your investment.

To test this assumption, your software developer would build the very first part of the portal: an online form that your customers can use to enter in their order. The form sends an email containing the order to your sales team and, at the same time, an automated email to the customer, thanking them for their order and letting them know that one of the team will be in touch if they have any questions. Now your sales team has more time to follow up those orders when there are complications or questions, as they're not deciphering emails, asking standard questions that are missing from those emails or being waylaid by customers phoning their orders through, disturbing them from their current work.

As you test your order form, you'll quickly find out what additional fields to put in it so that your team has the right information every time without having to ask for it. You can integrate features on the form repeatedly to make it better, to ask the right questions or to improve the language of the questions that your customers find confusing (analytics software can tell you this – more on that later).

You'll also find out what your customers think about using the form – if there's any reluctance and why. This process will teach you how to pitch the idea to your customers and help you to try different versions of the form to see if one works better than others. If you find that there's no way at all of getting your customers to use an online portal to place their orders, and they insist on ringing or emailing them through, then you're early enough in the process to pivot without having to rewrite the system.

This is the Lean methodology, described beautifully in Eric Ries's classic book *The Lean Startup* (2011). Lean is the art of testing for feedback with the smallest piece of work possible, iterating on that work to improve the feedback, and then testing again.

When you're deciding on what to automate:

- Select the most important assumption to test.

- Build the smallest amount of software to test that assumption in the wild.

- Iterate on that software to find the optimum way of solving the problem you're aiming to solve and to ensure that the assumption is fully tested.

- Repeat.

The MVP is small enough to test various iterations of the assumption in the wild. Testing these early assumptions with a much larger piece of software is risky, as changes would be more complex and time consuming to make. Testing the MVP at the first stage ensures that your initial assumption is good or allows you to keep trying ideas until you find a way to make it work.

You then have confidence to test the next most important assumption by expanding on the MVP. In this way, as my friend and colleague Jon Farrar once wisely pointed out, your software is *always* an MVP. You're only building the least you need to build to test your next assumption.

A misconception about the MVP

There's an important and common misconception that I'd like to clear up before we go any further. When you're creating your MVP, while we're talking about building the smallest possible piece of software to test your assumption, it's essential that the software is still perfectly formed.

By that, I mean you need to get your branding right. Make sure that the user interface (UI) is beautifully designed, the UX is as good as it can be and the system performs as well as it can.

Your MVP cannot compromise on design, UX or functionality, but it needs to be only the smallest slice of the functionality you need to test your current most important assumption. Finding this line is harder than you might think. Let's use a simple example to show what I mean.

CASE STUDY

I was running a Clarity Workshop with a client. We'd already defined a clear use case for the software we were building and assumption to base the MVP on:

'We assume that our customers find it helpful to use this software to store their data.'

The client and her team are veteran tech entrepreneurs and had successfully innovated, scaled and exited businesses previously, using software to leverage their processes and impact. They totally get the concept of the MVP.

The challenge for most visionaries is that they see the whole picture, the whole vision of what's possible, and want it all in the MVP. Each feature is seen as essential to the project; one of my toughest jobs is keeping projects lean, only building features that are demanded by users, rather than building features the client thinks they'd like with no data to back that up and no assumptions tested. With this team, that was not a problem.

It was clear that the first version of the MVP was to be a piece of software that allowed the client's customers to record or upload their data, and then retrieve that data from a list or a search. Also in contention for the MVP was a series of AI tools that segmented, tagged, summarised and categorised the data to make the analysis of it easier and more intuitive.

The client, her team and I all agreed that the AI aspect wasn't essential for the MVP. We simply needed to know if the customers would use the app to store their data. However, a couple of days later, we each independently came to a new conclusion. The AI tools were indeed essential for the MVP as the customers weren't going to use the software to store their data unless it provided them with a way to easily access and analyse that data again later. Without the AI, the software had no real purpose.

We re-thought the AI element and the new vision of the MVP emerged. This improved our understanding of our target audience and allowed us to remove other elements from the scope that weren't necessary for the MVP because they didn't prove the key assumption. We finally had the *right* MVP scope with which to test our initial assumption.

When the MVP is launched with the fewest essential features, you then unlock a whole new level of insight: user feedback. Once the system is let loose on your team or your clients/customers (usually both), you'll soon find out what it needs. From user feedback, you'll be able to compile a list of new features to be put in place, and another list of improvements you need to make to existing features.

You'll also know whether your initial assumption was correct, and therefore whether it's something that you want to continue to build on. Before you launch, it's speculation; the earlier you launch, the earlier you can find out whether you're building what your business needs to take it to the next level.

Delivering in small interactions, learning from your customers' feedback and iterating on that feedback is a powerful way of building software. It reduces risk;

it also makes sure you build something that is going to deliver what you need it to deliver.

The features of an MVP

It's worth noting that an MVP isn't always a tiny piece of software – at Remote, we've built many large applications as an MVP. The key here is that it's always the minimum we need to deliver the specific outcome we're looking for.

For the developer, the process simply is:

- Define the problem we need to solve.

- Design a set of features that will solve that problem.

- Deliver the software that will provide those features.

We keep to this, just focusing on those features that solve the problem we need to solve. We don't stray from the path and add nice to haves that don't directly contribute to the outcome we've defined.

If my desired outcome is to remove the duplication between one system and another, a feed showing latest news or an email notification containing a report of how many times that duplication has been removed might be nice, but it doesn't directly serve the intended solution this time round. They may well be features we build into the next round, the next MVP, if they directly contribute to the new most important outcome.

You can let the ideas flow for your MVP, but if they don't contribute to the targeted outcomes, they belong to the project-backlog list. This is a list of all the features you might add to the system in the future.

Having a backlog serves two purposes:

- No idea is completely disregarded, and so you can stay in innovation mode, rather than switch your brain to 'no' mode.

- When you're on a later phase of your software build and need to provide a new outcome or respond to user feedback, you'll have a list of features to pick and choose from to find the best solution for the problem you want to solve.

The MVP keeps you focused. It keeps project phases fast and agile, reduces upfront costs on untested assumptions and allows you to deliver your project as quickly as possible to elevate a bottleneck or increase revenue. Then you can move correctly and do it again, knowing that what you've already designed and built is not sitting there, unused on a developer's hard drive, but out in the wild, working hard for you, saving and earning money and energy while you get on with more important work.

Consider and decide what will constitute your MVP. At this stage, that means deciding on the most important outcomes that you need to deliver. You can start at a high level at this point; in the next chapter, we'll get granular and begin to really define what's going to be built.

Scoping your application

You now know what bottlenecks you're going to tackle first, having identified the biggest concentration of frustration or slowdown in your business by mapping out the pain points in your customer journey. You've designed your new ideal customer journey and defined your MVP – the part of that journey that's in most immediate need of improvement using software.

This should give you a sense of a piece of software that will fix an issue, improve your workflow or increase your capacity. This is exciting; can you see how your business will improve as soon as this piece of software is built and in place?

Each phase of software development you undertake will be the next MVP – the level-up you build to prove the assumption that if you have some software to do x, then the result will be improvements in y. One of the biggest keys to success in your software development will be in getting the scope right – transferring the ideas and concepts in your head on to paper so that a competent software developer will be able to understand and implement them correctly.

There are two important things you need to get right here, which at first glance may seem to be contradictory:

- Be as specific as possible about the outcome you require.

- Be as unspecific as possible about *how* that outcome will be achieved.

What you're looking for is complete clarity at a fairly granular level about what the software needs to do, but not so much technical instruction that the developer has no freedom to bring their own expertise to the table and improve on your vision of how it might work.

A good software team will consist of strategists, UI and UX designers, front-end and back-end developers. Each brings a unique insight into the software development process. Through experience, study and trial and error, the team will have learned patterns, workflows and architecture that work well.

You are an expert in your industry, but the chances are that you have never built software before. Beautiful synergy and innovation arise at the intersection between your industry experience and that of the development team. Pushing the technical specs too far into your domain or, conversely, pushing them too far into the development domain without bringing your own experience into it will lead to an unbalanced relationship and an end result that isn't as good as it could be.

There is a difference between software development houses or agencies, and software development or digital product studios. An agency will need you to create a detailed list of features and a technical brief for its team to work to. A studio will work with you to develop those things to achieve the optimal balance we're talking about here.

Go back to your ideal journey map and pick out the section that you've selected to work on for your MVP. Get clear on what the outcomes are of this section of the journey and how they can be improved.

First, write down the assumption/s that you're intending to prove. By this, I mean what are you assuming you'll achieve if you build this software?

Here are some examples of assumptions:

- 'If I build a dashboard for my clients to show them the progress of the work I'm doing for them, they won't phone in to the business so often, so my call centre charges will be reduced.'

- 'If I provide an online system that takes customer orders and sends them straight to our delivery team, it will reduce turnaround time and free up my sales team to follow up on larger sales and build customer relationships.'

- 'If I can automate the majority of the conveyancing process for my customers, it will allow me to scale without hiring more staff and free me up from a lot of the paperwork I do now.'

- 'If I provide all of the key metrics for a specific industry in a single portal, then it will be a valuable service to provide to my existing customers or sell to new ones.'

Next, write down a list of the outcomes you're intending on achieving with the MVP. These will be in line with the assumption you've just written.

For example:

- A customer dashboard that displays the status of orders for customers

- A reports page that will allow our team to track and amend the status of orders

- A notifications system that advises customers by email whenever the status of their order is completed

Now that you have a definite set of outcomes, follow through your ideal journey map and write the list of features you'll need, noting them as you spot them on each step of the journey. For example:

- A customer login so that customer data is secure and private

- A customer dashboard that displays:
  - Current orders
  - The current status of each current order

- A page for each customer order showing notes and progress of that order, with current status and estimated delivery date

- A team area to manage order details and statuses

- A notification piece that sends each customer an email when the status of an order is changed

It can be challenging for business leaders to give in to this process. 'Now that I've thought of this feature, it *needs* to be in the MVP' is a common statement.

Take a moment to check your original list of outcomes when you think of a new feature. Will this new feature actively contribute to your intended outcome? More importantly, is this outcome unachievable if the feature is not included?

We're going to remain agile throughout the process, so you can be a little relaxed about your first list of features for the MVP. It isn't written in stone and will most definitely change as you learn more about the application during development. Your application scope will be your description of what you need to achieve your goals.

Working in this way makes sure that you're always clear what you need to achieve and why each feature is essential to the success of the project. It's also the best method I've found for reducing the curse of software projects: scope creep. This is when you keep adding new features to the project before it's released, and usually happens when there's not enough attention applied to the initial assumptions and outcomes, or the feature list is too vague and not kept strictly to those assumptions and outcomes.

Keeping to scope is much harder than you might realise. When you're in the midst of a software project, it can be exciting – features are being delivered, you're seeing new interfaces for the first time and everyone you show the WIP to has an option and an idea for another feature that could level it up. All of these views are valid, but they can soon knock you off-piste, and the focus of the project can slip, along with deadlines and budgets, if you don't stick to the method I've outlined here. With each new feature idea, ask the same questions – is it essential to prove the assumption and can you achieve the intended outcome without it at this point?

I'm not advising you to build anything half-baked, remember. The MVP should be functional, reliable, usable and beautiful. It should also only include the features that you need to achieve the outcomes the software is being built for. You work on the most important items first, ship as early as possible to get real-world feedback on what you're doing, and repeat.

A good development studio team will be able to take your list of features and use their expertise to turn it into a technical brief for the developers; a brief that takes into account the lessons of past projects, the abilities of the development team, and the latest practices and breakthroughs in the world of software development that will benefit the project. Use that and watch your MVP fly.

Outcomes vs output

You may have noticed so far that I've defined your end goal in terms of *outcomes*. This is an important distinction, as it can be tempting to slip into thinking of *output*.

The world of development can be obsessed with output – x many lines of code, x thousand followers on social media, x many pages on a website or x many tasks completed. Software projects often kick off with the development team being handed a large business requirements document that describes output: a page that does this, a button that does that, a function that manages this and so on.

Focusing on output in this way can be efficient; a development team just needs to get their heads down and complete the list of tasks. However, what it fails to take into account is the need for everyone to know *why* they're doing what they're doing, so that the results can be measured.

Imagine you want me to drive to a particular destination. You can simply give me the directions and if they're accurate, I can follow them, but if I hit road-works or an accident and I don't know where the end destination is, I've lost the ability to use my initiative and get round the obstacle. I also lose the ability to spot shortcuts or make improvements on your directions based on what I see when I get to certain milestones in the journey. I have no sense of anticipation or moti-vation based around what's going to happen when I arrive as I don't know what the destination is or why I'm heading there.

If you share with me the destination you're taking me to, along with why I'm going there, what it's like and what I might expect to see along the way, I am likely to be more motivated to use my initiative, take the odd available short cut or even choose a more effective mode of transport that improves on your directions and the time it takes to get there. By sharing the outcome you require from me, you're empowering me to use my own abilities to get there, based on my experience and knowledge.

What we're talking about here is efficiency vs effectiveness. To be efficient is to get as much done as possible within a certain time. To be effective is to have as much impact as we can within that time. Being effective means to understand what our end goal is and to choose the best tasks to achieve that end goal. We might get ten things done that make very little progress towards our end goal or we might complete two tasks that make a big difference to it.

This relates to software development because it's important to always work on the things that will have the biggest impact on your end goals. It's also important when you're working with a software development team to hold back as much as possible on getting super-specific about the actual output you need. Be really strong on the end result you're after and let the team use their experience to choose the best way of implementing that end result.

Describe what needs to happen, but not necessarily *how* it needs to happen. Put into the scope that the customer area must be secure, but you don't need to add that you want a login page with a blue button that says 'submit' and a smaller green link that says 'forgotten password', and the company logo needs to be top centre, and so on. It is much more powerful in this case to add to your scope:

- The customer needs to log in to the dashboard securely.

- The customer needs to be able to reset their password if they forget it.

- The customer needs to be able to log out, and so on.

Of course, this doesn't mean that you're not supposed to suggest your ideas or describe your vision; it just means that you give the whole team the opportunity to buy into that vision and put all of their resources to working with you to achieve it. It's a team effort; it's not all on you to work it out. Let the UX designer do their thing and create the best experience for the people who log into your app. Let the senior architects know how much you anticipate the system to be able to scale and what's needed in the short term, but leave them to design the architecture and coding patterns necessary to achieve that.

The more specific you get, the more you restrict the abilities of your development team to let their superpowers shine. That will almost always be to the detriment of your project.

By coming back to the outcome you're looking for, you can take shortcuts if you need to and build whole new roads when you see the opportunity. This keeps you agile, lean and much more likely to reach your destination with something that works well, is adopted eagerly and delivers your intended results.

9

Prototype

Now we know what our software system needs to do, it's time to figure out how it's going to work from the point of view of its users. Just as we did with the MVP in the previous chapter, this means getting the whole team on the same page about end results. Wireframes are a great way of doing this.

We will look at wireframes in more detail later on, but basically, a wireframe is a bare-bones drawing of your end application. Business leaders tend to leave the design of wireframes to the UX designers as this is their skill area. It's not designed, it doesn't usually use colour and is often done by hand or with specialist software, but if done well, a wireframe can ensure the project continues with the same collaborative energy as it starts with.

A wireframe will be a loose drawing of each screen in the application with buttons, form elements, menu options and so on, so that the UI designers and web developers can get a sense of what will go where and how the interface is likely to work.

Nothing is permanent, of course. The chances are that when the application reaches the design stage, the UX/UI designers might have a better suggestion for layout or flow between pages, but the wireframe will make sure that everyone understands what the features will be and how they might work.

The main source of tension that needs solving here is that a wireframe produced too early on can dictate a layout or design decision that's hard for a designer to un-see. For example, once I see a dropdown box performing a particular search function to bring back a list, I find it difficult to re-imagine another solution. Making decisions too early in the process can be costly, especially if you're not aware of the technical implications of these decisions.

On the other hand, your list of features can sometimes be too abstract. Despite your best efforts, your descriptions are open to interpretation.

Shaping

Ryan Singer is the head of product strategy at Basecamp, creators of legendary product management and internal communication software. In his excellent book *Shape Up: Stop running in circles and ship work that matters* (2019), he describes this tension and its resolution. The problem is that words are too abstract and wireframes are too concrete, so we need an in-between solution called *shaping*.

Singer writes:

'Over-specifying the design also leads to estimation errors. Counterintuitive as it may seem, the more specific the work is, the harder it can be to estimate. That's because making the interface *just so* can require solving hidden complexities and implementation details that weren't visible in the mockup. When the scope isn't variable, the team can't reconsider a design decision that is turning out to cost more than it's worth.'

This solution uses rough diagrams to describe what will be on a page or how a feature will work, without going into so much detail that you begin dictating layouts and design patterns with the drawing. It shows the designers and engineers what needs to be done, while leaving space for them to work their magic, coming up with effective solutions to the problems presented in the best way they know how. This saves project costs and prevents the team from falling down development rabbit holes.

'Despite being rough and unfinished, shaped work has been thought through. All the main elements of the solution are there at the macro level and they connect together. The work isn't specified down to individual tasks, but the overall solution is spelled out. While surprises might still happen and icebergs could still emerge, there is clear direction showing what to do. Any open questions or rabbit holes we could see up front have been removed to reduce the project's risk.'

At Remote, we use shaping when there's a particular problem to be solved or feature mechanism to be worked out. Thick markers on whiteboards ensure that nothing is interpreted as *design*; it's rough enough to communicate what we need without it dictating how anything should look or work.

If you use this method to communicate more abstract ideas with your development team, it can be part of a powerful process that avoids misunderstandings, saving time and money. Shaping should be a collaborative experience between you and your product leads. Keep the group small – you, the key digital strategist for the application and perhaps the senior architect, and lead UX/UI designer. Your aim is to agree how the users of your app should use the software – the flow, the order in which they'll do things and how they might access the key features. Keep as open as possible to ideas and suggestions, and agree up front that no suggestion is wrong or out of bounds.

Adopting a 'yes, and...' approach leaves everyone free to suggest ideas and gets creativity flowing.

Once you've explored all the ideas, you can refine and agree on the most intuitive approach for each feature.

A bonus of this exercise is that the key members of your development team will have a much clearer understanding of your ideas, and you'll have a much deeper understanding of how the application will work and what benefits you and your team will gain from using it.

Wireframes

With shaping in place to roughly describe the features and actions of each page or process, the design team members are more informed about what they need to accomplish and how features will work, while you haven't dictated interfaces, methods or layout specifically. This allows their experience and creativity to shine through.

The next step is to create the wireframes we referred to at the top of the chapter. The aim here is to establish input types – like buttons, text and dropdown – the layout of those inputs and the structural guidelines of the application.

A wireframe is usually black and white outlines, occasionally with shades of grey or filled-in buttons to determine things like primary and secondary inputs or achieve some differentiation. It's important to keep wireframes low-resolution; you're still not *designing* at this stage. The higher fidelity they are, the more likely you are to be concerned about spacing, colours and typefaces, when the focus at this point is UX.

Are the right things on each page? Is there a hierarchy that makes it obvious what the intention is of the page and how to achieve that? Is there a consistent pattern that means users intuitively know how to use the features on each page without having to turn to a manual or click random things to see what they do?

Business leaders sometimes like to draw the wireframes themselves. A common mistake I see happen at this point in the experience is it often leads to unconventional layouts or interface mechanisms that take some time for developers to work out and feel awkward. This is understandable; as visionaries, leaders want to push boundaries, but there's a balance to be had.

Internet software has been around long enough now to have established conventions and recognised patterns, and although there are differences in layouts throughout the software world, there are enough similarities for users to be able to use apps straight away when they open them up for the first time. If you leave your users pulling confused faces when they open the app, you're putting obstacles in their way.

When you get into a new car for the first time, although it may be a little different to your old car, things are in a familiar place. The steering wheel, dashboard and gear stick are within reach and you don't have to think too hard about how to use them. You're soon comfortable and driving intuitively.

This isn't because car designers are lazy and just copy each other; it's because conventions have been established. Those conventions make it easier for new drivers of a car model to adopt that model.

In the same way, the conventions of web applications allow us as users to feel familiarity right away. Logo at the top or top-left; clicking on it takes us home. Avatar on top right; clicking on it lets us log out, adjust settings or account details. Main menu at the top or the left. Search in the middle near the top. We have conventions for layout, with primary buttons most visible and performing the most common tasks (save and publish, for example). Secondary buttons are less prominent alongside them, performing important but less commonly used actions (like save to drafts).

Your UX designer will be aware of these conventions and will have developed their own patterns and workflows that they've tested and refined over years. This is why shaping is the best way to communicate your ideas, and a designer should then take those ideas and turn them into wireframes. Remember, you're not looking at interface design here, but layout, buttons and features that will show how the application will be used.

Your designer will most likely use a specialist application for the wireframes, something like Balsamiq, Miro, Figma, Sketch or Axure. Many tools used for wireframing allow the designer to make buttons and features clickable, so that you can click through the different parts of the interface as if you were using the end application to get a sense of how it will feel.

When you get your first set of wireframes back from the UX designer, go through each one from the start of the user journey. Imagine you're using the application, from log in to main dashboard. Go through the list of features in the application scoping document you've written for the MVP, asking yourself, 'How will I accomplish this feature?' Look at the wireframes, clicking on relevant buttons to achieve each task.

Time spent here will reap huge dividends further down the line. It's very common for people at this stage to simply glance at the wireframes and say, 'Yes, that looks good, let's see the designs now.' A more methodical approach will save designers and developers from having to go back later and rebuild or add in features that have been missed.

There's still no need to get bogged down in details at this point. Take a high-level overview, making sure that the structure works, the layout is intuitive and workflow is smooth.

Just to be clear here – there will be things that have been missed and features that need to be added in or changed. That's part of the process, but spotting misunderstandings or omissions now reduces to and fro between you and your developer later on, and allows you to ship earlier and faster.

The design stage

Things start to get real at the design stage of the process. You'll have a good idea by now about how your application is going to work and, most likely, what it will feel like, but nothing can beat the excitement of seeing the designs for the first time.

Using the wireframes as a reference for structure and layout of UI elements, the UI designer will create a high-fidelity mock-up of the application, taking into account your brand guidelines – typefaces, colours, design cues – and turning ideas for feature interface elements into fully designed screens. Essential at this point is creating a design hierarchy: rhythms, patterns, primary, secondary and tertiary colours and button styles. Your designs are initially likely to consist of individual screens, showing each stage in the customer journey and how each feature looks as it's used.

Designs are essential, as the nature of each one will encompass the tone and character of the application. Just swapping out the typeface can change a stern, aloof product into one that's welcoming and friendly. Different colour palettes will present different feelings; this is an important stage and will set the tone for the rest of the development.

It's worth spending some time before the design stage to get to grips with your end user's avatar. Imagine a key user of the software – be it a team member within your business or an ideal customer. Give them a name, a role; build up a back story. This gives you a good idea of the kind of character you need to present to them within the design interface. You're really deciding the tone of voice of your application.

Your designer will most likely present you with a selection of key pages, maybe the main dashboard and several inner pages, depending on the outcome that the application is aiming for. Enjoy the moment as you see what your application will look like. Then consider these questions as you look over the screens.

1. Does the design have the right feel?

Do the typography and colour scheme present the right message to your avatar? It's worth noting here that you don't need to be formal in your messaging or branding. Friendly and welcoming is popular, and with good reason – you want the users of your software to feel comfortable and welcome in your environment.

This is as true if your app is customer-facing as it is if it's for your team. If a piece of software is cold, aloof, authoritative or just clumsy or difficult to use, you'll get resistance to using it, and even if that resistance doesn't manifest in vocal complaints, efficiency and momentum will reduce.

Remember, the aim is to get your users into flow: that timeless and spaceless state where everything is effortless. They won't get there if they can't work out how to perform an action or the interface looks clumsy and ugly.

2. Does the layout have structure, hierarchy, rhythm?

This is a much more subtle observation, but your app should be clear on what the main aim of each page is, where your user needs to click and what they need to do. If you feel something isn't standing out enough, don't go back and ask the designer to make it bigger or bolder or brighter; you create contrast by taking things away, by making space, by setting some things back, much more often and effectively than by making something stand out more.

Consistency is essential. Components should have the same style throughout – if your primary button is blue with white text on one screen, it shouldn't be green with white text on another unless there's a valid reason for it. The same goes for all the interface components. Spacing between elements should be even and mathematically balanced. At Remote, we have a design system that uses space in multiples of eight – gaps between elements will always be 8px, 16px, 32px or 64px. Even a few pixels out can make an interface feel off, but it won't be immediately obvious why.

A good design will just feel right, in balance, without anything grating or seeming off. You'll be able to look at a page in an application and know exactly what you're supposed to do without conflicting options. It's a skill to get this right, which is why the selection of your design and development team is a very important choice. A good, experienced UI/UX designer will have tested and integrated on many patterns in their career, and will have improved with feedback from users in the real world. It's hugely helpful for you to take advantage of that experience.

3. Is the logo big enough?

Just kidding. Your logo's big enough, I promise. It doesn't need to stand out more or pop.

A key insight here is that your brand is not just your logo; it's your design patterns, your interfaces, your typefaces. The whole presentation of your application is your brand, so your logo doesn't need to shout. Just like people will recognise the Golden Arches from a tiny segment of them, look at a fraction of a screenshot from Dropbox, Airbnb, Facebook or Gmail, and you'll know immediately what app it's from and what company made it. That's the beauty of a consistent, considered design system.

The anatomy of a design system

Let's spend some time going into exactly what I mean by *design system*. Not every online application has a formal design system, but every one that does benefits from huge time and cost savings, and a much more consistent, useful and recognisable interface.

A design system is the single source of truth for an application interface: a collection of all the guidelines, assets, components, layouts and templates that comprise its design. Each component in the system can be used as a reference, so that as the development continues, it keeps the same look and feel. A design system will often contain the styling code or cascading style sheet (CSS) for engineers, so that they don't even have to think about how to style an element.

A complete design system defines standards, concepts and patterns of a digital product. When the system is well-defined and followed by the development team, the level of UX is greatly improved, and the application feels intuitive and looks better. Design systems improve and evolve as the product does, and as elements are updated, these changes can be filtered through to the application as it gradually morphs into the software your users need.

Brad Frost created his Atomic Design Methodology in 2013, and it remains a design system standard today. In his book *Atomic Design* (2013), he writes:

'Atomic design is not a linear process, but rather a mental model to help us think of our user interfaces as both a cohesive whole and a collection of parts at the same time.'

The main parts of a design system to consider are:

Structure. The structure of the system is defined by the components, templates and layout. These are the building blocks of the design system and should be considered as single elements that can be combined and arranged in any number of ways.

Elements are the basic building blocks of a design system. The atomic part of the system, they can be combined to form components and are designed and built for use within the interface. The elements should be able to be reused throughout the application, so that when you need to create a new component, it can be pulled from the existing library of elements.

Components are the combination of elements that make up the interface and can be used again and again. There should be a set of standards for each component, so that they can be used consistently and their look and feel can be updated over time.

Patterns. These are the standard ways in which components are arranged and used throughout the interface. They are the design rules that are applied to components and enable the interface to be predictable and consistent, while at the same time flexible and reusable.

Templates are the patterns of components that are arranged in a specific way, and are used to create the look and feel of the interface. They're the style guides applied to the components that help the interface to be consistent and easy to use and update.

Pages are the final top-level design element. A page is an individual instance of a template, with the content specific for that page alone. The content may include images, text, lists and other ways to display data – each new combination of data will produce a new page.

Frost (2013) explains:

'We must create systems that establish reusable design patterns and also accurately reflect the reality of the content we're putting inside of those patterns. Pages also provide a place to articulate variations in templates, which is crucial for establishing robust and reliant design systems.'

Allowing for variations is crucial. A list of data on a page could have 10 items and look perfect, but what happens when it's returning 100 items? A text element might look beautiful with 70 characters, but what about 250? Pages will define these differences, all using the same template, but with different data variations.

Typography, colour palette, tone of voice and iconography are other elements of a design system which set an aesthetic tone throughout the application.

Primarily, the design system should be created with UX in mind and designed to help your users find what they are looking for. All of the parts I've listed have a role to play in doing that.

Design system benefits

A design system is a simple yet powerful tool that can be used to great effect. It will help you to create a consistent, intuitive interface, while saving you a great deal of time, effort and money.

A design system allows you to develop the interface quickly with a consistent feel. It will also help to maintain consistency as the application is updated over time to reflect the needs of your users, ensuring that the updates are reflected in all areas of the interface. When the interface is updated, the design system acts as a reference to remind you of the guidelines for how it should look, so that it remains consistent and recognisable.

A design system will improve the UX by making the interface intuitive and easy to use. It will reduce the number of clicks and make the interface feel like a natural extension of the user's desktop. It will also make the interface consistent across the different platforms.

Building a design system in this structured way produces a language for an application and a guide for every instance of every page. Developers don't have to go back to the designers for tweaks to pages, and there's no ambiguity about what elements are right for a use case. As applications get bigger, this is invaluable, as different designers and multiple developers can all work on features and the interfaces will be cohesive and consistent; the design grammar, tone and interaction concepts will all follow the same pattern.

Not having a design system can lead to a loss of integrity within the app, costing you time as developers try to work out how a feature should work, look and feel, and money as changes and improvements are made that would have been right the first time if a system was in place. There are tools that allow you to build design systems – check the resource page https://paulmcgillivray.com/resources for an up-to-date list. What's essential is that you have a collection of components, guides and patterns that can be used by your developers to build consistent pages.

On the development side, turning a design system into a code component library is worth the upfront time investment. When one piece of code for every component is built once and used everywhere, if the design for any component needs to be amended, updated or improved, it will change that element throughout the application. For example, if user testing shows that a button needs more white space behind it or a different font, amending that single component style will update every instance of that button throughout the app.

One last thing about designs – remember, this is your MVP, which isn't a rough version of your future application. It needs to hold all the attributes of a full final app, but with a smaller feature set, so you don't tolerate scrappy designs here. Your designs must hold the promise of a piece of software that's functional, reliable, usable and beautiful. As far as your end users are concerned, the UI is the application – they can't see the code, the architecture or the infrastructure. If the design is half-baked, it will feel like your software is, too.

Mockups

Mockups are the next stage in the design process. This is where the Prototype step of SCOPE really comes into its own. Developing prototypes in the form of mockups requires consideration and planning but can be well worth the investment.

As I've already stated, until you put your application in front of your audience, be that your operations team or your customers, you're working on assumptions. You might feel that they're solid assumptions based on experience and your business strategy, but you're still assuming that your idea will work; that the proposed system will address bottlenecks or streamline processes; that your customers or teams will want to use the system; that the workflow you've mapped out is intuitive and efficient. Your aim is to test these assumptions as early as possible so that you can change direction with minimum cost if you've mis-guessed. You need to de-risk the project.

You may think of these mockups as a nice-to-have and be reluctant to pay for them to be built. Why go out and create a mockup when you already know what you want, and you've designed your interfaces so you know how it will look and work?

Over the years, the team at Remote has learned the answer to those semi-rhetorical questions. When a designer presents you with the interface designs, you look at the whole thing, take it on board, absorb the branding, the UI style, the feel of it. Your brain does a mental checklist for the main features and buttons, and if all is well, you give it the OK to proceed to development.

The chances are that you may not notice any downside to missing the mockup step. Except for one thing. It can easily be put down to other issues like bad communication or changing your mind, but if you skip the mockup step, the first time you get to actually click on things and make the app work – ie test the workflow to make sure everything is where it should be; that all the required functionality is in place – will be when that part of the application has been developed. At that stage, it's much more time consuming/ expensive to go back and change things.

It's many times easier and quicker to make a change before development work has happened than afterwards. Moving pixels in a design is much quicker than amending the interface by code. A clickable mockup of your app gives you the chance to do that.

Typically, this mockup will start with a set of high-level design ideas and concepts, just as we've discussed, which are then turned into working interfaces. These interfaces can be tested with end users who can give feedback on how easy the app is to use and whether they can find the information they are looking for.

This is the key difference – the end users will be able to give you feedback *before* you've built the thing they're giving feedback on. This takes the pressure off you and the development team to know exactly what your end users are thinking and what should work. You're not fortune tellers, so all of your assumptions need to be tested as soon as possible. This is what the prototype gives you.

There are myriad types of mockup. Here I'll outline those we use at Remote, as they're to my mind the most effective.

Feasibility prototype

A feasibility mockup is usually called a feasibility pro-totype. It will help you test the riskiest of the technical assumptions you've made. Can your system perform at the level that you need it to? Will this new way of sorting data or presenting it to the user or calculating or searching actually work?

At Remote, we refer to this as a spike – a techni-cal deep-dive into a particular problem to make sure that we know the best way to tackle it and that the proposed technical solution will work. Doing this up-front will dramatically de-risk the project and make the development process more enjoyable; there are few things that lower morale and restrict flow more than the shadow of a big technical challenge up ahead that could make or break the project. Spike the job, make sure it will work up-front, and the rest of the project is smooth sailing.

Low-fidelity mockup

Following on from the wireframes that you've already created, a neat and simple step forward is to make them clickable. Many online tools will let you create your wireframes, and then make connections between buttons, pages, dropdowns and popups so that you can use the app as it is intended to be used.

Putting this in front of your target user at this stage will give you great feedback on whether buttons and inputs are in the most intuitive places and the navigation works in a way that means things are where the user would search for them. User testing with low-fidelity mockups will catch obvious mistakes early and help you to identify missing features or clumsy workflows before you solidify the structure and layout into high-fidelity mockups.

High-fidelity mockup

This works just like the low-fidelity mockup, but the screens that you make clickable are pixel-perfect versions of what the final application will look like. At this point, the designer has fully developed the wireframes into a solid design system, with the interface elements crafted and created as if they were screenshots of the finished product. This gives you the opportunity to test the visual hierarchy and make sure that the design system works when it's transferred to multiple interactions.

The market for hi-fi mockup tools is huge, so you'll be spoilt for choice. At Remote, our favourite is Figma, as our designers can create the individual pages and component library and turn them into a clickable mockup to share with clients, so it's a low-friction, minimum-additional-work way of delivering quickly. Figma's Dev Mode means our developers can interpret those designs into code directly and create pixel-perfect interfaces.

Pre-sales

The main aim with mockups is to test them with users, even if you don't plan to make any changes to the design. This will give you an idea of whether your design is easy to use and can help to identify any usability problems before they reach the development stage.

There's another huge benefit once you get to the high-fidelity clickable stage: sales. If your application is going to be customer-facing, a new online service in the form of a SaaS platform or digitising an existing service, you can take your hi-fi mockups and start putting them in front of potential customers to bring in some pre-sales. At Remote, we advise our clients to do this whenever possible, and have had some excellent results.

CASE STUDY

When the Remote team was building a platform for a client who connects large companies with systems, applications and products contractors, the sales director was able to start selling while we were building. He landed several global corporations pretty quickly, purely from sharing the clickable mockups.

Having a huge retail chain as your first customer can be quite a motivator. We all knew from that point that we were on to something special and were able to build and iterate with confidence. When we launched the platform, it had a running start, and our client was able to get a significant financial investment fairly soon after launch to allow them to scale the business. They had traction from the start, so the platform showed real promise.

As I write this, another client has just started taking the mockups of their new environmental accreditation platform to potential clients. They've already landed several major companies, which has given them the confidence and resources to go ahead with the build.

If your application is an internal business management platform, your equivalent of pre-sales is team buy-in. People don't tend to like change, so getting your team members used to the idea of a new platform and a new way of doing things will take time. Mockups allow them to give their feedback during the build, so that they feel they're part of the process, not victims of it.

Involving the team and your potential customers in the entire user-testing process is essential. Let's talk about that process next.

User testing

This is another essential part of the process that is often skipped when deadlines loom. User testing can feel a little like a formality if you don't do it regularly, meaning that you continue not to do it, but with design prototypes, bringing in user testing early and frequently will save you considerable time, expense and frustration as your project progresses. It could also help you identify opportunities that you might otherwise have missed. Don't make the mistake of avoiding user testing; start thinking about it from the beginning of the project.

As visionary business leaders, we know what we want to build and can clearly see the path to armies of users loving our application. Our teams are in flow and doing valuable work, our systems are automated and capacity has increased. This is all possible, but we *must* check in with the end users along the way to test our assumptions. Yes, we may be wrong. Let's stop that from happening.

Ideally, user testing will happen when each feature is developed. Put it in front of the people who will be using it right away. Don't wait until the whole application is built; it's essential you get early feedback that will show you whether you're on track and begin to prove your assumptions right or wrong as soon as possible.

Waiting until the project is finished before user testing can be incredibly costly. A pointer from an experienced team member early on can avoid hours' worth of fixing later and uncover hidden gems in ideas and workflows that may not have come up during the Clarify stage. It's impossible to guess how the user will take to the software; watching them use it early on and listening to their feedback is key to a successful development.

Focus groups

Early user testing may take the form of focus groups. Get together six to ten potential end users – either team members or customers who will be using the application. Show them the designs, the mockups, and walk them through the concept and why you think the app will make their life easier. Ask questions and *listen* to the responses.

It can be really tempting to try to defend or explain your ideas if you come up against negative opinions. Do all you can to resist that temptation. Create an open conversation and welcome all thoughts – nothing's out of bounds. It'll be a waste of everyone's time if you bring in people who just want to make you smile and will only give you positive comments. Negative opinions are gold; they give you a collection of objections you need to overcome.

You can do this easily with sales content or framing, or by changing the way the application works. You can't do this easily if you don't know what those objections are. It's for this reason that it's useful (if challenging) to bring in customers or team members who can sometimes be naysayers. You want to unearth all the potential objections upfront; your onboarding can then contain content that explains or reframes the application accordingly.

Naysayers are your canaries in the mine. If they're fine and happy with the mockup, and they're the most difficult people to please, or if you can change their minds, you have a good, clear run going forward with others. Buy-in from teams is essential with internal projects, and focus groups are a fantastic way of bringing champions on-side – having influential team members leave the meeting and tell the rest of the team how exciting this new software is going to be will make a huge difference to your roll-out experience. People tend to hate change, even if it's change for the better. Champions will help your cause immensely.

Similarly, having the buy-in from clients as you build the system creates early adopters and pre-sold evangelists outside your organisation, which can start a buzz and provide organic marketing for you. You'll also know you're building something that will work for your clients.

One-to-one testing

Sitting next to someone as they walk through the mockups or prototypes (or in-progress application) is the next level, and is the heart of user testing. The best way the Remote team has found to do this is to get your ideal target customer or a team member who will be actually using the application and give them a list of tasks to perform. Then watch.

See where they get stuck; see where they ask for more context or information. See how easily they're able to complete the task. It can be helpful to switch a webcam on and record video of their facial expressions as they use the software; watching back to look for confusion or frustration, even if only slight, will help you to improve the flow as they work with the final application.

Pay particular attention to the user's instinctive reaction. If, for example, they need to change something in settings and they go straight to the top right to click on their avatar (the common place for settings in apps), but the settings option is in the left menu instead, it will throw them off. Cues like this are real gems and could be a pointer to move the settings to the place where users are already looking for them.

Doing these kinds of tests regularly, preferably after each significant feature is first designed, and then developed, will give you confidence, guidance and motivation to continue, knowing you're on the right track, and the option to make important changes before you release to your main audience.

Post-launch

User testing can really ramp up once you've launched the application and it's getting real use from team members and customers in the field. There are some great apps that can collect usage data and give you feedback on how the application is being used.

I've included a list of the Remote team's favourite prototyping, mockup, testing and user feedback tools on our website at: https://paulmcgillivray. com/resources.

With the prototyping step complete, you can be sure that your software will be well-received by your target audience. Your assumptions have become certainties. Now you're ready to move with confidence on to the final stage of the SCOPE framework, and here's where things get real.

You're going to execute on your creation.

10

Execute Part 1 – Understanding Your ROI

B y now, you should be getting a sense of what software could do for your business, and perhaps
how much time you could save or your capacity for
taking on work could be increased. It's going to start
getting exciting now, but there's likely to be a nagging
question in the back of your mind – or maybe the fore-
front – that I want to address right now before we go
any further:

'How much is this going to cost?'

It's rare that this isn't the first question I'm asked
by clients as soon as they realise the benefits a software system can provide them.

When you do software wrong, 'cost' is the right
word. It can cost you big-time with little return. If
you do it right, it's not even a cost; it's an investment,
and one that can bring big dividends. How do you

know which side of that all-important fence you're going to find yourself on? Choose the right team to design and deliver your software, but before that, you need to know what you want to achieve financially, and work back from that to calculate what you need to build and how much you can spend to get to that goal.

Let's say you have a team or department of ten people, earning the business £560k per year. You pay each person £40k per year on average and have expenses of £9k per month, totalling £108k per year. That leaves a profit of £52k annually.

You can see that you're at capacity at this point (you can't perform any more work with this number of people). Your solution is to either hire more staff or improve the effectiveness of the team. You choose effectiveness.

Why effectiveness and not efficiency? Efficiency indicates a measure of how quickly a task can be done with the least amount of energy. No matter how efficient a team member is, if they're working on the wrong task, it's useless to the overall goal of improving profit. Busyness does not directly relate to profitability. If a team member is effective, the work they're doing is making a direct difference to your goals.

Using the TOC and customer journey mapping we discussed in earlier chapters, you see that the bottleneck to increasing capacity is in the delivery part of your business. Sales is bringing in more work than delivery can handle, and customer service/support is managing its workload with no problems, and even has some capacity. Naturally, the first and most obvious thing to do would be to bring a team member or two from customer service over to delivery, but you want to ensure that the remaining support team continues to delight your customers, so this is a first aid measure that contains some risk.

Your ideal is to increase the capacity of the delivery team by automating tasks and freeing up team members previously doing those tasks. If you can't completely automate any tasks, then using software to streamline the workflow of the people carrying them out can be equally useful.

Say you have seven people in your delivery team. Each team member completes fourteen units of work per two-week cycle. At £375 per unit, that brings in £5,250 per cycle. Twenty-four cycles per year means that each delivery team member earns £126k annually; they cost the company £45k each in salaries and taxes:

£126k × 7 = £882k income − (£45k × 7) = £567k profit

If you estimate that after you've improved the workflow using software, each team member can deliver an additional two units of work per cycle, then the total number of units delivered per cycle would increase from 7 × 14 = 98 to 7 × 16 = 112. To calculate the increase in income resulting from this extra productivity, you can use this formula:

Increased income = Number of additional units per cycle × Price per unit × Number of cycles per year

Using our example numbers, we get:

Increased income = (14 × £375) × 24 = £126k

To calculate the ROI of the software:

ROI = (Benefit − Cost) / Cost

In this case, the benefit of the software is the extra income that results from the increase in productivity of your delivery team. The cost of the software is the amount you paid to purchase it.

Plugging in the numbers from our example, we get:

ROI = (£126k − Cost) / Cost

For example, if the cost of the software was £120k, the ROI would be:

ROI = (Benefit − Cost) / Cost
= (£126k − £120k) / £120k
= £6k / £120k
= 0.05

This means that the ROI of the software for the first year is 5%. It basically pays for itself after a year.

The increased income after five years would be £630k, which is calculated by multiplying the annual increased income of £126k by five. Take away those initial software costs of £120k and a 17.5% support and maintenance fee of £21k for the following four years, and you'll get a total profit of £426k over the five-year period for just over 14% improvement. That doesn't include the additional profit gained from team members you may add during that period, so you're setting yourself up for more leverage on any scaling you undertake.

That's a simple overview of one way to analyse the costs. Here are the main factors to consider.

- **Factor one: Time savings.** When you introduce new software into your existing processes, tracking how long tasks used to take with manual methods versus how quickly they can be completed with the software is an important calculation. Let's say that before you implemented a custom system, it used to take eight hours for team members to complete a certain task manually. After the implementation of the new system, it only takes two hours – that's a 75% reduction in time and cost. If you're paying a team member £15 per hour, it's costing you £30 to complete that task instead of £120; a saving of £90 each time it's done.

  There's an important flip side to time savings. If a team member only takes two hours to perform a task that perhaps earns the company £400 where it was taking them eight hours before, that means that they can now perform that task four times within the same period. They're earning £1,600 rather than £400 in the same time, so you haven't just saved £90, you've earned £1,200 more.

- **Factor two: Cost savings**. Implementing a custom workflow system can help businesses reduce expenses across the board, from personnel costs to financial losses arising from mistakes due to streamlining processes. This can bring about substantial cost savings for your business. I had a client losing 10% of their stock due to mistakes made by manual processes, which was costing them at least £200k a year. A system to reduce these mistakes saved costs significantly.

  Without a custom system, businesses often spend hundreds or even thousands per month on subscriptions to third-party platforms to get the job done. This cost adds up, especially if using this software takes time and is prone to error thanks to the difficulties involved in managing multiple systems.

- **Factor three: Revenue increase**. Improved customer satisfaction, higher efficiency or better productivity created by implementation of the new software can all increase revenue. Customers remain loyal because their orders are fulfilled on time and they may even make additional purchases – leading to more profits for your business.

- **Factor four: Efficiency gains**. It's important to look at efficiency gains as well as cost savings. When processes become more efficient, they also become more cost effective over time – which is exactly what you'll want out of custom workflow software. If improved efficiency leads to increased revenue or faster turnaround times, then this could bring larger profits.

There's another, invisible, factor that's often overlooked when business leaders are calculating whether to invest in new software: future targets. If you're turning over x and you have a target of y in five years, you need to think about the bottlenecks in your current systems and the effectiveness of the resources you have. How will you meet these targets? If you increase your leads and conversions, do you have the capacity to deliver at the pace you'll need?

Often, the choice is to add more people to the mix. Of course, this works to a certain extent, but if the processes aren't effective, you're adding more inefficient workers to your team, with all the additional resource and communication overheads that go along with that. Optimising your systems first means that when you do add more people, each new team member is leveraged many times and your ROI is higher, too.

Elevate the bottleneck first and make all your processes as effective (or completely automated) as possible using software. Then, if it's necessary, add more team members to an optimised workflow. You'll be able to analyse your team journey to find out what the bottlenecks are and map a new journey to uncover a solution using the processes we covered earlier. That will tell you whether software is key or it's time for more people.

If you need to spend more time building relationships with clients or doing work that involves creativity, empathy, moving or arranging things, or other only-human attributes, then people are the answer. For everything else, there's software.

Deliver with confidence

You're probably not a software developer. By now, I'm sure you can see the benefits that software will bring to your organisation, but there is likely to be one burning question in the back of your mind as you read this book:

'How do I build it?'

The quality of your development team is an essential element in the success of your project. The difference between the right and wrong team can be the difference between saving, earning or losing tens, even hundreds of thousands of pounds – perhaps millions.

Don't panic, I've got your back. The next sections will guide you through your development options and we'll discuss the difference between an agency and a studio, so that you can make sure you pick a development partner that can do the job brilliantly in the way that is right for you.

Who do I get to build this thing?

Building software is not to be taken lightly. Done well, it can transform your business and allow you to reach new customers, give your team more freedom and autonomy, increase your margins and scale beyond your dreams. Done badly, it can cause frustration, set back your plans and cost a huge amount of money.

This is a book about software development, but I haven't shown you how to code. Your job isn't to write the software, but to commission the right team to take your obstacle, aim, vision, and turn it into something that will elevate your business to the next level.

Most of Remote's clients fall into one of two categories:

1. They see the potential for a software solution to remove a bottleneck, streamline a workflow, allow them to scale or roll out a new service, but need a development partner to take the next steps.

2. They've already been through a process with a software developer and have been stung – the software didn't work and had to be scrapped, or it just about worked but had so many bugs or such a terrible workflow, it caused frustration with team members and customers. Perhaps the development team ended up building something different to what was needed.

Following the steps I've outlined so far in this book in collaboration with a good software development team, you will dramatically reduce the chances of the latter happening to you. You'll be clear on your vision and what's needed, and be able to communicate this to your development team. You'll have a good working prototype that allows you to test the concept with your team or customers before work has started on the code. This can be used to let programmers know exactly what's needed. You'll also know what assumptions to test and prove up-front before you've built the whole project.

The aim of this book is to give you a real sense of what should happen at each stage, so you're not left feeling vulnerable and having to simply trust what you're being told. You'll have the big-picture knowledge to have confidence in making decisions when you need to, which will greatly contribute to not only the success of the project, but your enjoyment of the process. That's important too, right?

You have three choices:

1. Build your own software team

2. Utilise existing software platforms

3. Find a software development agency or studio

Later sections will give you a clearer idea on what would be my suggestion. First, though, let's have a delve into history.

The Skunk Works

During World War 2, Lockheed Martin – a leader in the defence industry – was commissioned by the US Air Force to design and build a new jet fighter to counter the increasing military threat in the air from Germany (Lockheed Martin, 2020). Most of the Lockheed staff were busy working on a new bomber, commissioned by the British government, so to meet the requirements, the Lockheed leaders did something new and unusual.

They tasked engineer Kelly Johnson with picking a small team to secretly design and build the fighter. Kelly realised that if his team was to meet the innovative demands of the new jet within the budget and timeline required, he was going to have to work outside of the usual Lockheed processes and bureaucracy. As a result, he moved his team outside of the organisation's premises and set them up in a circus tent on the outskirts of a plastics factory.

The team members were given autonomy to try new ideas, free from the usual red tape. In doing this, Kelly ensured they became agile and creative. They delivered their solution, the P-38 Lightning, within budget and with seven days to go on the deadline.

The project was such a success that the department, named the Skunk Works in reference to a popular comic book of the day, prompted by the malodorous smell emanating from the plastics factory nearby, still exists today, albeit in its own building rather than a circus tent. It has created at least twenty-two aircraft for Lockheed since the creation of the P-38, including the famous U-2 spy plane, the F-117 Nighthawk Stealth bomber and the F-22 Raptor (Lockheed Martin, no date).

Why did it work?

As an organisation grows, each new team member adds lines of communication and things can get out of hand quickly. Tasks get forgotten or confused and momentum can be hard to build; with no processes in place, research is repeated, creation becomes ad-hoc and the company struggles to evolve and learn from its mistakes and successes.

The natural (and correct) solution to this issue is to document and enforce processes, and build systems to allow for greater communication and easier workflow. However, at a certain point of evolution, those processes can begin to slow the organisation down. A decision that might be made in a few minutes within a small team can take six months within a corporation, thanks to the sign-off hierarchy and the huge number of potential outcomes and consequences that the decision may create.

Going back to basics and splitting off a smaller team allows the organisation to go into start-up mode, freeing it from regulations that may have been put in place to prevent an issue that is no longer relevant, and allowing each decision to be made quickly by the person closest to the reason for it. With a stripped-down set of processes and each team member having the autonomy to work within their own superpower and make their own decisions (in line with the aims and values of the team and project, of course), the progress of a project can be dramatically speeded up. It can also nurture greater creativity and innovation.

The downside of the Skunk Works approach

There's one potential problem with this approach. Organisations with momentum have their own team culture, processes that work, methods for learning and building on that learning, and a language between team members that takes time to develop.

As Peter Theil discusses in his landmark book *Zero To One*, it's way more difficult to build something from nothing than to iterate on something that already exists (2015). This is why large organisations are much more likely to acquire a new piece of technology by consuming a smaller company than simply creating their own version.

For example, Facebook could have easily created its own version of Instagram; it had massive resources and engineering talent, but Instagram was up and running, had a huge user base, and the team (of only thirteen people) had momentum and a culture that worked. Instead of copying the application, Facebook bought Instagram for just over $1billion in 2012 (BBC News, 2012). Facebook went on to repeat the strategy, acquiring Oculus for $2bn (Meta, 2014) and WhatsApp for $16bn (Meta, 2014) in 2014.

Building a new team from scratch is hard. You need to create culture, agree on processes, find the right people who can work together and bounce ideas off each other and, in the case of software development, establish common technology and patterns to allow multiple team members to work on a piece of software in a way that can be maintained and scaled. All this on top of knowing what roles to hire and determining who the right people are for those roles.

The solution

This is the reason why so many business leaders prefer to outsource development work to a software development company. A small agency already has momentum, experience in building what needs to be built, a common language, the right people in the right roles, and a reliable set of processes that have been tried and tested already with previous clients.

When you outsource to a team to build your platform, you're hitting the ground running. You're starting from one, not zero.

There's one challenge with the software agency model. Most software agencies require a technical brief to work from, and building that technical brief requires a lot of expertise as well as a deep understanding of the needs that the software is aiming to meet. Many companies hire an external consultant to create this brief, but this third party often means that there's a disconnect between the requirements and the solution. Some software agencies can build a brief for you, but that tends to be a proposal based on the technical solution that the agency wants to build. Again, there can be a disconnect.

An agency is also focused strongly on software development. Its team is unlikely to have designers and product managers working collaboratively with you from your original idea through to launch. The relationship is more transactional.

The software studio model is subtly different. When you work with a studio, you get all the 'starting from one' benefits of an agency, but the team works as if they're part of your company. The emphasis moves away from 'What else can we suggest this company builds?' towards 'What should we build to solve the problem or meet the need in the most effective way?'

It's a step up from consultancy, a step towards collaboration. The conversation moves from 'you' or 'us' to a collective 'we'. With a studio approach, you start from the idea, and then work with the experts in the studio to create a vision of what the software could do. From that, you define an MVP, using all the tools and techniques we've covered so far in this book.

A studio also has designers and product managers in-house as part of the team, providing you that holistic offering. The studio team members will have been part of all the thinking, bringing their expertise and experience to the project, as if your company had an innovative in-house software department with the autonomy, agility and speed of the Skunk Works.

A studio collaboration is a move from transactional to relational communication. It's a step from a short-term project to a long-term mission. When you're thinking about the long game, the developers aren't concerned about pushing particular features because they will earn the studio more money; they're concerned that the software will meet your needs because a successful company means a continued relationship. That is profitable for everyone.

A studio might have a smaller team of engineers than an agency, but they will focus on developing beautiful and user-friendly software. Studio teams also often have expertise in UX, design, branding and marketing.

Of course, I'm biased, but with good reason. Remote was an agency for a long time, but because at our core we're interested in collaboration and long-term relationships, we naturally moved over to the studio model without even knowing it was a thing. Suddenly, we realised there was a name for what we were doing and were happy that others were doing the same.

Now we've fully embraced the studio model, we have even moved away from hourly or daily billing towards story-point and subscription-style collaborations that remove the stress of 'Am I near my budget yet?' I'm not recommending this approach because it's how we do it at Remote, but letting you know we do it at Remote because it's the best approach.

Why not simply hire your own in-house team?

You could easily look at a quote for a project with a studio and calculate how many developers and designers you could hire directly for a year with that money. I used to have the odd client bring this up back in the early days, before I was able to clearly articulate the benefits of a studio.

Rather than pay a studio to build your software with you, you could certainly hire a couple of mid-level developers for a year instead. The challenge here is twofold. A strong, capable, well-rounded software development doesn't just rely on a developer. You also need a project manager, scrum master and UI/UX expert, let alone a CTO – if you can find one. A good CTO would most likely take up the whole budget of a couple of years' development and will almost certainly already be working for another exciting company.

Then there's the big one – knowing who to hire. How do you know that the people you're bringing in are actually any good or can work together or have complementary skills? These issues arise before you even begin to build processes and methodologies and patterns and infrastructure.

Start on your own and you start everything from scratch. This means becoming a software company – building a team, creating and iterating on processes, learning quality control, patterns, infrastructure, architecture. All this while building on the actual product or service you started the company to deliver.

When software is your product, it's your main focus, your industry. You live and breathe it. When you're in another industry and you need to bring software in to allow you to scale and be more efficient, no matter how experienced you are in your current industry, that speciality will not help you to build a software team. That's a new set of skills – you're back to zero.

That's why we at Remote do what we do, and why collaborating with a solid, talented, process-driven software development studio is the best way to unlock the potential that your company holds. The studio creates and maintains your systems, and you can – yes, once more – get on with the work you're supposed to be doing.

Not all software studios are created equal. It's essential to do your homework and select a studio that not only has the technical expertise and experience, but communicates well and has proven methodologies to uncover the real obstacles to momentum and scale, and put solutions in place to make your business soar. The right studio will feel like an extension of your own team, working with you to deliver a solution that propels your business forward.

Existing software – the options

As you've probably seen by now, the software you leverage in your business can make or break your ability to run a cohesive, motivated team, scale and ultimately achieve your goals. Your choice of software isn't just a small operational decision; it's a strategic one that can significantly impact your company's future. The wrong choice can lead to unnecessary expenses, inefficiencies or, worse, stunted growth.

Working with a studio isn't the only option for getting your systems built. It may be that you don't need to commission a team to code your software from scratch. You or they may be able to utilise an existing solution to solve a particular problem. It's worth investigating those options before committing to a custom development, even if it's to solidly rule them out before stepping forwards.

While I've declared my bias and preference upfront and covered the main options in this section, it's important that you explore the potential advantages and drawbacks of all options to help you identify the solution that will best align with your business's unique needs and goals. It's not a one-size-fits-all decision; choose the right option for where your business is right now.

Off-the-shelf systems and SaaS platforms

These are ready-made solutions designed to cater to a wide range of businesses. They're most likely where you'll start on your business journey.

The fast-food equivalent of the software world, off-the-shelf systems and SaaS platforms offer quick and easy solutions. With user-friendly interfaces and low initial costs, they're perfect for companies looking to get up and running quickly. They're pre-built, so they're readily available for you to use immediately. Popular examples include ActiveCampaign for CRM or Trello for project management.

The initial cost of these systems is lower than that of custom-built solutions. This makes them an attractive and obvious option for businesses with tight budgets or a simple problem to solve.

Many off-the-shelf systems pride themselves on their user-friendly interfaces, making them easy for your team to adapt to. If you do run into problems, there's often a vibrant community offering support when you need it. If you have a problem to solve that's experienced by most businesses in your industry, the chances are that there's a piece of software available that you can use to ease that burden. The more widely the problem is experienced, the more likely there's software to help you with it.

Accountancy and bookkeeping, CRM, mailing lists, email – these are tools most if not all companies need these days, and so there's going to be a huge amount of relevant software to choose from. In many cases, it doesn't make sense to customise software for these tasks; why build a package to manage your accounts when Xero, QuickBooks or Sage already exists and can do the job out of the box? Look at what's available when you first turn to software to help run your operations.

Despite the convenience, off-the-shelf systems do come with their limitations. The most obvious and impactful is the lack of customisation. These systems are designed to cater to the masses, so they may not perfectly fit your business's specific needs or unique processes.

I call these 'fixed systems'. You may find yourself having to adapt your operations to fit the software, rather than the other way around. You'll also find that every business is different and soon you'll need multiple pieces of software running in tandem to meet your unique needs. At that point, you'll likely be looking at implementing a tool like Zapier or Make. com to synchronise data between systems. This can get messy fairly quickly, so it's something to keep an eye on.

The cost, while initially low, can grow over time as you add more users, more features and more systems. You may even find yourself paying for features that you don't use. Using off-the-shelf systems means placing a significant portion of your operations in the hands of a third-party provider. If the provider experiences downtime or decides to change their pricing or features, your business is directly impacted and you usually find you have no choice but to absorb whatever change has been made.

It's important to recognise that you don't have the IP rights to the software with third-party systems. If you're looking to build a unique competitive advantage or have a vision of exiting or securing investment, not owning the IP of your core business software may be a disadvantage.

Generally, your journey will be that you start with off-the-shelf software systems, but as the business grows in size and complexity, you'll find that they don't meet or resolve the bottlenecks you experience. Often, it's that very software that's causing the bottlenecks. It's at that point you need to explore other options, be it custom software or a highly configurable platform architected by a skilled team – the no-code or low-code platform.

Low-code/no-code platforms

The DIY toolkit of the software world, low-code/ no-code platforms have been improving their abilities over the last few years and are now a viable option for the more systems-capable operator. These platforms empower non-technical teams to build their applications, making the software creation process more accessible than ever.

The main allure of low-code/no-code platforms is that they democratise the development process. These platforms are especially useful when you're looking to build straightforward software systems that fit your business domain perfectly, but without the upfront cost of custom software or the restrictions imposed by generic off-the-shelf systems.

However, the complexity and customisations offered by these platforms can sometimes be limited, and you may face scalability issues as your business grows. You're still dependent on the third-party provider as these are SaaS platforms, and while you don't need to be a coding prodigy, designing a usable project still requires a degree of technical knowhow. That said, you're holding a lot of that knowhow in your hands right now, so a low-code/no-code platform could be a great way to start implementing what we've covered in this book.

There's a big place for low-code/no-code platforms in the world of business operations. If you can find the right platform with the right features/abilities, and get a team of knowledgeable experts to configure or customise it so that you're not compromising on your business workflows, scalability or outcomes/goals, then it could be a great step up from forcing your processes into fixed systems without needing to go all in on a custom system.

A good low-code system can work as an evolving system: one that adapts and changes with you and your business as it grows. If you choose to go with this route, my recommendation would be to form a partnership with a knowledgeable studio that can go through all the scoping processes I've covered in this book and configure and maintain the platform for you. If you're able to work with the developers who built the platform, then you may be able to commission customisations or additional features so that the system perfectly matches your needs.

I've included a list of the best low-code and no-code platforms for business operations in the resources guide https://paulmcgillivray.com/resources. Remote's own low-code platform for business operations – Autm.io – is on that list. We've integrated all of the patterns, components and solutions that we've developed for different projects over the years, including those listed in the 'Optimal Journey' chapter of the book, so they can be configured precisely for your business domain and specific challenges.

Autm will allow you to deliver quickly on the solutions you will uncover while following the SCOPE process. You can use the Scorecard at paulmcgillivray. com/resources for immediate guidance on whether to choose SaaS platforms, low-/no-code solutions, or custom software, so that you can get going with your software systems right away.

Now that you know how to get the best ROI from the software available to you and what the main options are, it's time to move on to the second part of the Execute step of SCOPE. We're going to look at the all-important skill of being agile.

11
Execute Part 2 – Agile

I n February 2001, high in the Wasatch mountains of Utah at a ski resort named Snowbird, a group of pioneers of the world of programming gathered for a summit that would define the course of software development. The result was the Agile Manifesto (Highsmith, 2001), and its principles show no sign of abating.

The manifesto and its accompanying principles are a declaration of culture and values more than anything else. No programming jargon is used; nothing is unapproachably academic. The manifesto puts people first and describes a fully human way of working that allows for the development process to be much more intuitive, responsive, free-flowing and – yes – agile.

I was introduced to Agile and its use in software development by Bob Marshall a little over a year after the manifesto was written. Bob is one of the world's leading experts in developer motivation and behaviour, as well as being one of the first Agile coaches and CEO of the first 100% Agile consultancy in Europe. We spent two days together covering the theory and implementation of Agile and another game changer – the TOC, which we talked about in the 'Strategy' chapter.

What Bob taught me over those two days improved my company's performance tenfold and set the Remote team on the right course. We started hitting deadlines. We delivered higher quality projects on time and on budget. We've continued to incrementally improve on those processes ever since.

Agile is plain talking, simple, collaborative and respectful. When working to its principles, we keep the big vision in mind, but deliver in small, perfectly formed bursts of immediately released deliverables, rather than a single release at the end of a long development. Thanks to Agile, each project we've built has been an improvement on those we've built before it. Our clients enjoy the development process, and the Remote team lives and breathes their dreams to make them a reality in a culture of harmony, mastery and technical excellence, leading to sustainable software development.

When people talk about Agile, remember that it's not necessarily about the processes. It's about the culture, values and intent of the declaration.

Agile in the real world

The Agile manifesto intentionally leaves a lot of room for interpretation. Each framework gives a different take on achieving its aims, but in the main, an Agile development looks like this.

Development runs in cycles of anywhere between one- and six-week iterations (two is the most common). A high-level vision of the intended result is discussed and described, but granular planning is left as late as possible, usually carried out during the cycle before the one in which the work is due to be carried out. The end result is held loosely and is open to alterations during the development as business needs change and user feedback is received.

The project is developed in small vertical slices, rather than large horizontal slices – so a feature is delivered end-to-end in an immediately usable format, rather than all the infrastructure, then security, then database, then back-end architecture, then front-end interface. Doing the former allows for much faster feedback times compared to the latter, where the application can only really be used when the whole thing has been developed. Often, it's then that stakeholders discover the developers have misunderstood the requirements, and the project needs to be scrapped or large sections rebuilt.

With Agile, work tickets for the developers are created from the end user's point of view in the form of user stories, rather than describing technically what needs to be done. A user story will take the form of 'As a [user type], I need to [describe need] so that [describe reason]'. For example: 'As an administrator, I need to be able to add, edit and remove stock items from my inventory so that I can keep track of my products available'. This provides a strong and unambiguous goal for the developer to work to, while giving them the freedom within that framework to add their own value and genius to the project. The addition of 'definition of done' to a ticket lists a set of variables defining when the work meets requirements.

Agile teams are small and cross-functional. This means that rather than having all the designers together, the front-end developers somewhere else and the back-end team in a huddle in another building, each team consists of multiple disciplines. There will generally be a designer, a front-end developer and a back-end developer – sometimes the team is larger, maybe two of each of the developer types up to a maximum of six people, but the key is that the implementers of the entire product development lifecycle work together as a unit on each feature.

Key stakeholders are included in the project as a single team. This leads to strong collaboration and a much-reduced chance of the developers misunderstanding the requirements. It doesn't mean that the stakeholders code or design the project; they're simply involved in key meetings on a regular basis to discuss what work needs to be done and how it will be implemented.

Every part of the project contains automated tests, written in code, that form a scaffolding around the whole. Whenever a feature is built or deployed, the tests are run, and if a single test fails, the deployment is halted.

This means that developers can build with confidence and even dramatically change the architecture of a project, knowing that if all the tests pass, they've not unwittingly broken something else – a common occurrence on medium-to-large projects. The best teams build their tests first, and then write the code to pass the tests. This method – known as Test Driven Development – requires a certain mindset from developers but increases the chance of a solid and reliable project, and keeps programmers focused and less likely to fall down rabbit holes.

Transparency is essential in an Agile project. The team members do all they can to be open about progress, velocity, end products and any issues they've encountered, so that the stakeholders know exactly where everything stands. This leads to the last – and my favourite – feature of Agile: no surprises.

When the final application is delivered and launched, it's often barely even noticed. There's rarely a 'ta-da!' moment – no big reveal – because those who it's revealed to have usually been part of the process at every step and the project has launched gradually in small stages from very early on in the process.

As a software development studio owner, I do sometimes find my ego longing for the old days of saying, 'Here you go!' and receiving praise for a project launch, but to be honest, it's a much greater reward for the project to slip fully formed, gracefully and gradually, into the real world, rather than making a grand entrance that may be met with dismay if something isn't right. 'No surprises' means everything has gone as expected and a good job has been done by all.

As you can see, Agile end results go a long way to describing an ideal situation for software project development. It requires discipline to fully adopt it, but once Agile is in place, projects get completed faster, deliver what they promised and are fun to partake in.

The big bang vs iterative improvements

There's a reason that Agile is such an important set of principles and values. It's a reason that's most easily seen when you examine the alternative.

Software developments are often seen as a one-off project – scope it, build it, install it and get on with the rest of your business. We at Remote refer to these as 'big bang' projects. They tend to take on a Waterfall management process and are very unwieldy to build.

The difference between Agile and Waterfall is night and day. Waterfall tends to be a result of the project owner needing to set a fixed scope, budget and timeline for a project. Unfortunately, these projects usually end up being over scope, over budget and delivered way beyond their deadlines.

This is because the project owners are forced to make early assumptions about what the business needs, what problems they're solving and how they're going to solve them. They do this for a whole bunch of problems, build a big piece of software to solve those problems, but as the project progresses, they learn more about the problems, and find more problems within the proposed solution and others to be fixed that they didn't know about at the beginning.

They then release their solution in full to a team, only to find the software's been built without a full awareness of the team's needs and workflow. Cue new features, amendments to existing features and the need to find more budget.

With Agile projects, you develop in continuous iterations, releasing features as you build them and taking on board user feedback as the project continues. It's a series of iterative developments, rather than a big bang.

With Waterfall, the moment you stop developing your software, it begins to date. Your business moves on, usually at an increased pace thanks to the new system, but with no one continuing to work on the system to improve it alongside the business, it will fall behind and become the bottleneck instead of being the thing that elevates the bottleneck.

The installation of a system can actually change the requirements of the system. New ways of performing tasks will reveal different obstacles or frustration points. This is a good thing if you have a practice of continuous improvement. What you're doing is revealing opportunities to speed things up and increase flow and momentum in the business. A task that operated more quickly than another now seems slow because the other task has been removed or sped up. In other words, the faster task is the new bottleneck and needs the attention of the system.

The adoption of a new system will also change the way things are done. This is an intention, not a side effect. Be ready for these changes and respond with improvements and adjustments that nudge the flow in the right direction. See what features are being used the most and get feedback from users about what they don't like, what doesn't work for them and, conversely, what they think is great, so you know what to add more of.

This is a continuation of the user testing you did during the Prototype stage of SCOPE and should be an ongoing process. Software years are like dog years – a year in the real world is the equivalent of five to seven in software terms. Framework versions increase, new ways of doing things are developed, technology best practice moves on.

I'm not advocating for constantly changing infrastructure or frameworks or patterns just because there's a new one, but new versions can offer performance improvements and features, and keeping up with them can make it easier to add features in the future. Look at it like car maintenance. Back in the day, I'd never service my car and did the bare minimum I needed for it to pass the annual MOT. After a few years, breakdowns were regular, performance was down and I noticed my MOTs were increasingly expensive, until eventually the cost of repairing the car was higher than replacing it, so I scrapped it.

I'd done this in multiple iterations since my first car, until about five years ago when I bought a car that I really love. Because I love it, and bearing in mind all the previous cars I'd driven into the ground and scrapped, I decided to give it a full service every year, and to fix and tweak any issues the mechanic noticed ahead of the MOT.

As a result, I've never broken down in that car, it still runs brilliantly, and my MOTs and services are always way less expensive than they used to be. This is common sense for cars, and it should be common sense for software development, too.

Often, a client will come to Remote with a piece of software that hasn't been maintained since it was built, and now slows down the whole company. Once upon a time, that software was the saviour of the company. Now the client needs to scrap it and start again.

With an Agile development, good architecture and ongoing maintenance, the relevant features can be added when they're needed, as soon as the feedback comes in. With regular services – framework upgrades, refactoring, reindexing etc – better performance features can be implemented, and even more complicated amendments like changing the data layer to a different database provider, for example, can be done without you having to scrap your software system and start again.

Leave it once it's built, and five or so years later, the chances are that you'll need to pay for an expensive rebuild. You would also have lost performance in your team during those years that the software wasn't performing as it should have been.

When you're building everything up-front, you don't have the opportunity to find out what your customers or team members think of the features you've dreamt up until they've got the whole thing in front of them. A feature that you might have considered a must-have may, in reality, be of no interest to your end user or have a fatal flaw which ends up making the whole system frustrating or impossible to use in the real world. This is dangerous, as these kinds of mistakes can be expensive.

You can protect against this in part by making sure that you're using real use cases as your examples to build out your feature set – solve real problems with your software that you've uncovered with your journey mapping. That takes us right back to Strategise, the first stage of SCOPE. However, there's a bigger problem with the big bang method. In making all the decisions and creating all the features before you've put the software in front of your end users, you're missing out on the opportunity to use them as a resource for innovation.

The people using your product day-in and day-out will have a unique insight into how it should work. Doing all the thinking before they get a chance to help means not only do you have a higher risk of getting it wrong, there's also less chance of coming up with something unique that takes the whole product to the next level.

The sooner you get your software in front of the people who are going to use it, the quicker you can check that you're on the right course. The longer your feedback loop, the higher risk you're taking with your project.

CASE STUDY

A medical storage provider was facing significant data management challenges with their manual archiving processes. They partnered with Remote to develop a secure, cloud-based application tailored to their needs. Over several years, we continuously improved the system based on feedback from customers and the internal team.

The initial project focused on providing an intuitive way of managing the data archive. Our team worked closely with the client to understand their unique requirements and build a system that met their exact needs. Over time, we added features and refined the application to enhance functionality and usability, ensuring it evolved seamlessly with the company's growth. This allowed the client to scale from £1m to over £16m in annual revenue before exiting to a large global company.

By taking a customer-driven approach, we ensured the system remained robust and adaptable. This gradual, steady improvement streamlined operations, contributing significantly to the client's impressive growth and successful exit.

This underscores the power of incremental improvements and highlights how continuous,

customer-driven development can create robust,
adaptable software solutions that support significant
business growth.

An aeroplane is much more likely to reach its destination if the pilot checks its orientation constantly, rather than every hour or, worse, once they think they should have arrived. A good pilot checks their orientation, adjusts and checks again continually, until it's time to land.

That's a great model for software development and one we run at Remote. When you're developing software, I strongly suggest you or the team you work with use Agile principles too. Be a good pilot and you'll get exactly where you need to go.

Conclusion

I 've talked a lot about software replacing the tasks that don't require human elements such as relationship building, empathy, compassion, creativity or intuition. Humans are best at human things. We crave expression and connection, and when we're unable to express ourselves or experience that connection, our lives can feel empty and unfulfilled.

In the orchestration of the human with the digital, we have an opportunity to let technology take over those parts of our work that don't make us come alive. That don't allow us to be creative or to build relationships or to learn or to craft or to love. To suggest that our work might offer us this opportunity almost feels alien in a society where many of us pre-millennials were brought up by our parents to find a good stable career that would earn us a solid income and to stick to it, whether or not it makes us feel fulfilled or allows us to have a meaningful life.

As humans, we thrive when we're doing work that has meaning. The evolution of our societies from cave-dwelling nomads to city-dwelling globalists connected by an invisible web of technology didn't happen overnight or as the result of just one magnificent and super-intelligent person. It's the result of billions of tiny improvements and ideas and acts of creation – many of them almost imperceptible on their own, but together and over time, they are the giant leaps that allow us to live how we live today.

Despite what is insinuated in the news, at this time in history, humankind is experiencing fewer wars than we have for thousands of years, less extreme poverty and more opportunities than ever before. Yes, humanity faces bigger challenges to our future than ever before too, but if we look at how far we've come in tiny incremental steps, carried out by all who have gone before us, we can see that we have a part to play.

Each of us is unique. We each have a combination of individual talents that mean we can and must excel in a particular area that is unique to us, and we won't do that by performing mindless administrative tasks. We do that by letting software become our sidekick that supports us while we make our tiny but essential difference in the world.

Steve Jobs once described the evolution of technology as being like a rock. If you cut it clean down the middle, you see that huge, heavy rock was built by layers and layers of sediment, each one a tiny increment added to the last (McBurney, 2013). Our own impression on the world may be gone and forgotten in a decade or 100 years, but we leave our layer of sediment for the next layers to build on. We don't have to be the entire rock. Our task is to lay down our own unique expression for others to follow and lay theirs on top of.

Technology enables us not only to do this, but to increase the amount that we leave for the next pioneers to step up. At the same time, we're not starting from scratch – we stand on the shoulders of the many pioneers before us.

In the process of making our difference, we find meaning in our lives and find our purpose. This makes life more enjoyable, more worth living, happier, more flowing, and in many ways, we become better people along the way.

This is the true gift of software to us. I wish you clarity, momentum, fulfilment and adventure on your own software journey.

References

Apollo11Space, 'IBM's System/360: The groundbreaking mainframe that helped land men on the Moon' (no date), https://apollo11space.com/ibms-system-360-the-groundbreaking-mainframe-that-helped-land-men-on-the-moon, accessed 21 August 2024

Apple, 'iPhone X technical specifications' (2017), https://support.apple.com/en-us/111864, accessed 6 May 2024

Apple Documentation, 'iPhone 14 pro-technical specifications' (no date), https://support.apple.com/en-euro/111849, accessed 5 May 2024

BBC News, 'Facebook buys Instagram photo sharing network for $1bn' (10 April 2012), www.bbc.co.uk/news/technology-17658264, accessed 5 May 2024

Čapek, K, *Rossum's Universal Robots: A fantastic melodrama in three acts and an epilogue* (Doubleday, 1923), available online at https://gutenberg.org/files/59112/59112-h/59112-h.htm, accessed 17 June 2024

Computer History Museum, '1965: Moore's law predicts the future of integrated circuits' (no date), www.computerhistory.org/siliconengine/moores-law-predicts-the-future-of-integrated-circuits

DHL, 'Strategy 2025' (2019), https://group.dhl.com/en/about-us/the-group/strategy.html, accessed 17 June 2024

DHL, 'How digitalization has transformed DHL Express' operations' (2021), https://lot.dhl.com/how-digitalization-has-transformed-dhl-express-operations, accessed 17 June 2024

Ferriss, T (@tferriss) 'What would this look like…' (23 October 2023), https://twitter.com/tferriss/status/1716441791195423084?lang=en, accessed 2 May 2024

Frost, B, *Atomic Design* (2016), https://atomicdesign.bradfrost.com, accessed 17 June 2024

Gantt.com, 'What is a Gantt chart?' (no date), www.gantt.com, accessed 2 May 2024

Goldratt, EM, *The Goal: A process of ongoing improvement* (North River Press, 1984)

Goldratt, EM, *It's Not Luck* (Routledge, 2002)

Hanlon, M, 'Apollo Guidance Computer sale highlights contrasting views of historical significance', *New Atlas* (23 May 2017), https://newatlas.com/apollo-guidance-computer-dsky-space-memorabilia/49631, accessed 21 August 2024

Highsmith, J, 'History: The Agile Manifesto' (The Agile Alliance 2001), http://agilemanifesto.org/history.html, accessed 6 May 2024

IBM, 'The IBM System/360: The 5-billion-dollar gamble that changed the trajectory of IBM' (no date), www.ibm.com/history/system-360, accessed 21 August 2024

Jordan, J, 'The Czech play that gave us the word "robot"' (2019), https://thereader.mitpress.mit.edu/origin-word-robot-rur, accessed 17 June 2024

Kanban Tool, 'History of Kanban' (no date), www.kanbantool.com, accessed 2 May 2024

Kurzweil, R, *The Singularity is Near: When humans transcend biology* (Duckworth, 2006)

Landau, P, 'What is Lean manufacturing?', *Project Manager* (8 August 2023), www.projectmanager.com, accessed 1 May 2024

Lockheed Martin, 'The P-38: When lightning strikes' (2020), www.lockheedmartin.com/en-us/news/features/history/p-38.html, accessed 17 June 2024

Lockheed Martin (no date), www.lockheedmartin. com/en-us/who-we-are/business-areas/ aeronautics/skunkworks.html, accessed 6 May 2024

Lutkevich, B, 'Systems thinking', *TechTarget* (2007), www.techtarget.com, accessed 30 April 2024

McBurney, S, *Steve Jobs: Visionary entrepreneur,* documentary (2013)

Meta, 'Facebook to acquire WhatsApp' (19 Feb 2014), https://investor.fb.com/investor-news/ press-release-details/2014/Facebook-to-Acquire-WhatsApp, accessed 5 May 2024

Meta, 'Facebook to acquire Oculus' (25 March 2014), https://about.fb.com/news/2014/03/facebook-to-acquire-oculus, accessed 5 May 2024

Miller, M, 'The rise of DOS: How Microsoft got the IBM PC OS contract', *PC Magazine* (12 August 2021), https://uk.pcmag.com/operating-systems/135023/ the-rise-of-dos-how-microsoft-got-the-ibm-pc-os-contract, accessed 6 May 2024

Mori, E, 'The calculator that helped land men on the Moon', *IEEE Spectrum* (21 May 2019), accessed 21 August 2024

Pennington, C, 'We are hardwired to resist change' (Emerson Human Capital Consulting, 3 April 2018), www.emersonhc.com, accessed 30 April 2024

Priestley, D, *24 Assets: Create a digital, scalable, valuable and fun business that will thrive in a fast changing world* (Rethink Press, 2017)

Randolph, M, *That Will Never Work: The birth of Netflix by the first CEO and co-founder Marc Randolph* (Endeavour, 2019)

Ries, E, *The Lean Startup: How constant innovation creates radically successful businesses* (Portfolio Penguin, 2011)

Shirriff, K, 'A computer built from NOR gates: Inside the Apollo Guidance Computer', *Ken Shirriff's Blog* (September 2019), www.righto.com/2019/09/a-computer-built-from-nor-gates-inside.html, accessed 21 August 2024

Singer, R, *Shape Up: Stop running in circles and ship work that matters* (Basecamp, 2019)

SXSW, 'The singularity is nearer, featuring Ray Kurzweil' (2024), www.youtube.com/watch?v=xh2v5oC5Lx4, accessed 17 June 2024

Theil, P, *Zero to One: Notes on startups, or how to build the future* (Virgin Books, 2015)

Tilbury, C and Priestley, D, 'Millionaire starts from scratch: How to get rich starting with $0', *Strike it Big Podcast* (8 February 2024), https://strike-it-big.simplecast.com/episodes/daniel-priestley, accessed 17 June 2024

Acknowledgements

Jeannie – your love, strength, guidance and collaboration in every aspect of our lives have made me the man I am today, and the man I continue to become. This book wouldn't exist without you.

Ella – wise, creative, powerful and strong, you consistently strive to realise your own potential with truth and honesty at your core – and inspire me to do the same.

David – a brother, supporter and loving friend. Thank you for always being there, including throughout the creation of this book. Your insights have been invaluable.

With thanks to the Remote team members past and present, and the countless clients we've worked with, learned with and made a genuine difference in the world with. I couldn't imagine doing anything else for a living and am continually grateful for everything that Remote is and stands for.

The Author

Paul McGillivray is a seasoned entrepreneur with an extensive track record spanning over twenty-five years. As co-founder and CTO of Remote, an award-winning software development studio, he leads a team of diverse experts who design and build applications that streamline processes and scale businesses. Having spearheaded projects creating enterprise applications for global brands like Sony, Volvo, Volkswagen Group and Tesco, Paul excels in digital transformation, adept at turning complex challenges into clear, actionable strategies.

Passionate about integrating technology in a people-centred way, he influences business leaders to leverage their values and tech for growth and positive impact. On this theme, he's delivered keynotes all over the UK, including TEDx and B1G1x, is a co-author of the best-selling B1G1 book *Legacy* and is the host of the *Purpose First* podcast, as well as a regular guest on many business podcasts.

Paul's work displays a unique talent for explaining complicated concepts in a way that is easy to understand, and people leave his writing and presentations inspired and moved to use tech in new ways to make a real difference in their lives, businesses and the world.

⊕ https://paulmcgillivray.com

⊕ https://remote.online

▣ www.linkedin.com/in/paulmcgillivray

◼ www.facebook.com/paul.mcgillivray

▣ @PaulMcGillivray

◎ @paul.mcgillivray

🎤 https://paulmcgillivray.com/podcast